# Food in World History

Providing a comparative and comprehensive study of culinary cultures and consumption throughout the world, this book examines the globalization of food, illustrating how the diffusion of crops contributed to population growth and industrialization, and exploring the political, social and environmental implications of our changing relationship with food.

Including numerous case studies from diverse societies and periods, *Food in World History* examines and focuses on:

- the use of food as a tool of colonialism in Africa and Asia
- the influence of the Italian and Chinese diasporas on US and Latin American food culture
- how food was fractured along class lines in the French bourgeois restaurant culture and working-class cafés
- the results of state intervention in food production and distribution
- how the impact of genetic modification and food crises has affected the relationship between consumer and product.

This concise and readable survey not only presents a simple history of food and its consumption, but also provides a unique examination of world history itself.

**Jeffrey M. Pilcher** is Associate Professor of History at the University of Minnesota. Author of *¡Que vivan los tamales! Food and the Making of Mexican Identity* (1998), he has also published essays in the *American Historical Review*, *The Americas* and *Food, Culture and Society*.

# Themes in World History
Series editor: Peter N. Stearns

The *Themes in World History* series offers focused treatment of a range of human experiences and institutions in the world history context. The purpose is to provide serious, if brief, discussions of important topics as additions to textbook coverage and document collections. The treatments will allow students to probe particular facets of the human story in greater depth than textbook coverage allows, and to gain a fuller sense of historians' analytical methods and debates in the process. Each topic is handled over time – allowing discussions of changes and continuities. Each topic is assessed in terms of a range of different societies and religions – allowing comparisons of relevant similarities and differences. Each book in the series helps readers deal with world history in action, evaluating global contexts as they work through some of the key components of human society and human life.

**Gender in World History**
Peter N. Stearns

**Consumerism in World History: The Global Transformation of Desire**
Peter N. Stearns

**Warfare in World History**
Michael S. Neiberg

**Disease and Medicine in World History**
Sheldon Watts

**Western Civilization in World History**
Peter N. Stearns

**The Indian Ocean in World History**
Milo Kearney

**Asian Democracy in World History**
Alan T. Wood

**Revolutions in World History**
Michael D. Richards

**Migration in World History**
Patrick Manning

**Sports in World History**
David G. McComb

**The United States in World History**
Edward J. Davies II

**Alcohol in World History**
Gina Hames

**Childhood in World History**
Peter N. Stearns

**Religion in World History**
John Super and Briane Turley

# Food in World History

Jeffrey M. Pilcher

Routledge
Taylor & Francis Group

NEW YORK AND LONDON

First published 2006
by Routledge
711 Third Avenue, New York, NY 10017

Simultaneously published in the UK
by Routledge
2 Park Square, Milton Park, Abingdon, Oxon OX14 4RN

*Routledge is an imprint of the Taylor & Francis Group*

© 2006 Jeffrey M. Pilcher

Typeset in Garamond 3 and Gills Sans by
Keystroke, Jacaranda Lodge, Wolverhampton

Every effort has been made to ensure that the advice and
information in this book is true and accurate at the time of going
to press. However, neither the publisher nor the authors can accept
any legal responsibility or liability for any errors or omissions that
may be made. In the case of drug administration, any medical
procedure or the use of technical equipment mentioned within this
book, you are strongly advised to consult the manufacturer's
guidelines.

*Library of Congress Cataloging in Publication Data*
Pilcher, Jeffrey M., 1965–
  Food in world history / Jeffrey M. Pilcher.
    p. cm. – (Themes in world history)
  ISBN 0–415–31145–4 (hardback) – ISBN 0–415–31146–2 (pbk.)
  1. Food–History. 2. Food supply–History. I. Title. II. Series.
  TX353 .P46 2005
  641 .3′009–dc22                                    2005007198

*British Library Cataloguing in Publication Data*
A catalogue record for this book is available from the British Library

ISBN 0–415–31145–4 (hbk)
ISBN 0–415–31146–2 (pbk)

For my Mother, who introduced me to a world of food.

# Contents

# Acknowledgments

Thanks to Masaya Arakawa, Warren Belasco, Donna Gabaccia, Raymond Grew, Paul Gutenberg, Keith Knapp, Anne Rubenstein, and Sydney Watts. I also appreciate the encouragement of Peter Stearns, Victoria Peters, Philippa Grand, and the expert staff at Routledge. The Citadel Foundation, Charleston, SC, generously supported my research.

# Introduction

Everyone requires the same basic nutrients – proteins, carbohydrates, vitamins, and minerals – yet human societies have adopted wildly different approaches to satisfying these physiological needs. Agrarian peoples kept healthy on vegetarian regimes of up to 80 percent starchy grains, while Inuit hunters of the Arctic once lived almost entirely on whale meat – perhaps the ultimate in high and low carbohydrate diets. However monotonous these traditional food habits may have seemed on a daily basis, they collectively illustrate the range of cultural adaptations that have taken shape over the course of world history. The rise of modern, industrial societies during the past three hundred years has increased personal choice while narrowing the overall diversity of human food supplies, just as novelty diets and individualistic eating habits have undermined the sense of community formed over the dinner table.

The material constraints of environment, technology, and physiology set boundaries for human diets, but even traditional societies have been quite skilled in exploiting available resources. People obviously cannot hunt whales in tropical highlands or harvest grain from the Arctic ice; nevertheless, peasant farmers possess a tremendous range of practical knowledge of microclimates to maximize the harvest from any given field. The material nature of food, especially its perishability, likewise determines availability, although a society's technological base can compensate for such limitations. The use of refrigeration to keep food without spoiling may well reflect a modern failure of culinary imagination. Traditional preparations such as sausage, jam, pickles, and cheese demonstrate the technological achievements of earlier civilizations in preserving meat, fruit, vegetables, and milk. Even human physiology can adapt, over millennia, to overcome material shortages. Northern Europeans and Asian steppe nomads, unable to obtain sufficient vitamin D from sunlight alone, evolved a lifelong tolerance to lactose, unlike most humans, who can only digest milk, and the vitamin D it contains, in childhood.

The study of culinary cultures must consider both the material nature of ingredients and the beliefs and practices about these foods. India and Mexico provide a revealing comparison of two nations that eat largely vegetarian diets, use legumes extensively as a substitute for animal protein, and season generously with chiles and spices. Wheat flatbreads (naan) even resemble corn tortillas. Despite these striking parallels, structural differences run deeper. Mexican cooks consider chile peppers the indispensable foundation of a *mole* sauce, rather than simply one spice among many in a curry. South Asian meals consist of a variety of dishes served simultaneously, in contrast to the Hispanic sequence of courses. The social meanings of food diverge further; Mexican elites achieved distinction by monopolizing limited meat supplies while Indians preserved caste purity by abjuring meat. Historical perspective magnifies this contrast between the non-violence of Jain devotees and the ritual sacrifices of Aztec priests.

Commensality, the sharing of food and drink, forges bonds of group identity. Daily meals shared around the family hearth accumulate intimate and enduring social ties. Metaphors also link food to sexuality, further cementing the foundations of family life. In modern times, as communal meals have declined in regularity, symbolic occasions such as Thanksgiving and Christmas carry even greater emotional weight. Ceremonial feasts have also served to convey an element of familial intimacy to political relationships, bolstering ties between rulers and subjects. Moreover, the sharing of food habits helps to define ethnic identity, for example, through the Hebrew adherence to kosher dietary restrictions. The Christian Eucharist likewise illustrates the religious significance of commensality, linking humans to the divine.

Attention to historical change is essential to understanding how foods have helped shape human societies. The most basic associations of culinary identity, including Irish potatoes and Chinese tea, are historical artifacts – often of surprisingly recent vintage. Tea did not become popular in China until the Tang dynasty (618–907 CE), and no Irishman ate a potato, of South American provenance, before Columbus's voyage. Transformations in food production, from the rise of agriculture and pastoralism to the Columbian Exchange and industrialization, have had profound social repercussions. Population growth from the successive introduction of new plants, animals, and technologies has transformed economies and social classes. Changes in food processing methods also profoundly affect gender relationships.

The methodologies of world history, in particular, lend themselves to examining such fundamental trends. Admittedly, until the advent of steam power, only the elite consumed exotic delicacies or imported spices. Most foods eaten by most people were grown in nearby fields and orchards or were caught in familiar forests and streams. Yet even those "local" plants and animals may well originally have been domesticated on the other side of the planet. The exchange of foodstuffs has been a significant form of contact between civilizations for thousands of years. World historians have therefore devoted attention to the processes whereby new ingredients and cooking methods are incorporated into existing culinary systems, and to the cross-cultural exchange of attitudes toward diet and health.

Comparative research, another focus of world history, is equally important for analyzing the development of food production and eating habits, especially when looking at the transition to modernity. Westerners have often assumed their own culture to be uniquely proficient in technological and economic progress. Considering non-Western reactions to French haute cuisine or to McDonald's hamburgers, for example, can provide a useful corrective to such exceptionalist narratives.

Nevertheless, care must be taken in choosing appropriate samples for comparative analysis. In a synthetic volume such as this one, the most fully developed comparisons have been adapted from the work of distinguished scholars, whose publications are cited at the end of each chapter. Yet because the history of food and society is such a new area of study, the present work has necessarily ventured a number of hypotheses, with supporting cases selected largely on the availability of secondary works. The use of comparative methodology has been eclectic, although hopefully not promiscuous, with the primary goal of keeping cuisine grounded in its larger social and historical milieu. Each chapter has sought to examine at least three or four well-studied but far-flung regions of the world. Global inequalities of academic resources have made the book more Eurocentric than would be ideal of a world history. Readers may also imagine alternative case studies, which could yield quite different conclusions. With luck, the questions posed and the juxtapositions suggested between Western and non-Western societies will encourage future research in this vibrant subfield of world history.

Five historical themes stand out as crucial in shaping human eating habits, the first of which is the ongoing diffusion of foodstuffs. A handful of grains, most notably rice, maize, and wheat, now dominate global agriculture. A few common stimulants, including coffee, tea, chocolate, sugar, and spices, likewise are grown in tropical plantations around the world. Taste preferences have become equally global; chile peppers, domesticated in the Americas, now add piquancy to cuisines from Eastern Europe to Africa and South-east Asia. The mechanisms for this diffusion have been complex. While merchants have transported unfamiliar plants across continents and oceans, cultural knowledge of farming and cooking techniques carried by migrants, whether voluntary or forced, has been equally important in spreading foods. Emperors and smugglers also appear in the history of plant diffusion through their efforts to make and break monopolies on valuable crops. Ordinary eaters likewise determine the course of food history through their gut reactions of approval or revulsion. Evaluating the results of this crop diffusion is equally problematic. The triumph of high-yielding grains has significantly increased overall agricultural productivity, but at the cost of greatly diminished biodiversity. By betting the future on a few "miracle seeds," which may prove unsustainable, modern agribusiness risks the loss of humankind's precarious food security.

A second important theme running through world history is the tension between agriculture and pastoralism. Farmers and herders generally live in separate environments, with the former preferring well-watered lands and the latter dominating more arid regions, but frontier zones in between have been the site of ongoing competition. The rise of the Roman and Chinese empires brought agrarian civilizations to ascendancy, but imperial decline allowed nomadic German tribes and Mongol hordes to reclaim pastures from the plow. Dietary differences exemplified their radically different lifestyles; the nomads' carnivorous appetites symbolized their barbaric nature to more sedentary neighbors. Yet cooperation has been equally common, and the exchange of animal products for grain and alcohol offered a mutually beneficial trade. In the early modern era, absolutist agrarian states again gained the upper hand throughout the Eurasian heartland, but the opening of immense new pastures in the Americas and Australasia tilted the balance back toward a new industrial pastoralism. Cultural conflicts remain prominent in the contemporary world, for example, as modernization programs in developing countries attempt to convert herdsmen into farmers – devastating both people and soil in the process.

Class distinctions also arose historically through the distribution of food as well as other sources of wealth. In agrarian societies, balanced on the edge of subsistence, simply having enough to eat was a mark of high rank. Skeletal remains indicate that nobles in ancient Egypt and Mexico often stood considerably taller than their subjects as a result of better diets, particularly their greater access to protein. The consumption of rare spices and other exotic foodstuffs provided further distinction for classical elites. As food supplies became more secure in the modern world, the wealthy defined new and more subtle forms of exclusion based on refinement instead of bulk. In the diet-conscious contemporary world, obesity is correlated with lower-class status.

Other forms of social identity have likewise been shaped by food habits. Gender roles within any given society derive largely from the division of labor in preparing food and from the allocation of consumption within the family. Patriarchal societies tend to assign women the task of everyday feeding. When men do cook, they usually prepare high status dishes, large cuts of roast meat, elaborate haute cuisine, or ritual food for the gods. Men also generally claim larger portions and leave less-prized foods to women and children. Yet however devalued women's work may be within a society, their mundane tasks of daily cooking convey forms of power within the family. The customary foods shared by a cultural group also help forge the personal relationships that make up ethnic identity. Conversely, the physical repulsion often felt toward unfamiliar foods can exclude outsiders in a particularly visceral fashion, hence such slurs as "frog," "beaner," and "dog eater."

A fifth and final theme in this book is the role of the state in determining the production and allocation of food. Archaeologists have speculated that the accumulation of surplus food facilitated the rise of archaic states, as local chieftains used agricultural wealth to recruit followers and expand their political power. Governments, in turn, gained legitimacy by assuring that their subjects were adequately fed. Markets shared in the task of provisioning, which caused tension between political authorities and economic interests. With the advent of modernity came a belief that markets functioned more efficiently than governments in preventing subsistence crises – a proposition that has met with mixed results historically. Regardless, state power has not diminished noticeably in the past two centuries; indeed, ruling classes have discovered new means of wielding power through food, for example, by consciously fostering national cuisines as a means of winning popular allegiance to newly formed nations.

By exploring these five themes, this book traces the influence of food in the global transition to modernity. The first chapter sets the stage by describing pre-modern culinary systems within the Eurasian heartland. Comparisons between the agrarian empires of classical China and Rome focus on natural resources, culinary systems, social relationships centered on production and consumption, and attitudes toward the state as a guardian of food security. During the post-classical age (roughly 500 to 1500), Islamic cooks blended Mediterranean and Asian cuisines to form a new synthesis, not only mixing crops and cooking techniques but also combining farming and herding cultures.

Part I examines the origins of culinary modernity during the early modern era (around 1500 to 1800). Chapters 2 and 3 consider the global realignment of food production resulting from European expansion. The Columbian Exchange introduced highly productive crops from the New World to the Old in return for livestock and pathogens, causing demographic shockwaves in both hemispheres. This process was not only asymmetrical in nature but also uneven in speed and scope, offering historians revealing case studies in cross-cultural exchange. Notwithstanding the significance of grain and livestock transfers, an even greater influence on modern diets came from the spread of sugar plantations in the Americas. Within a few centuries, sugar overtook spices as the primary focus of long-distance agricultural trade, before eventually challenging staple grains as the very cornerstone of human diets. Modernity entailed other dietary transformations as well. The third chapter in this Part seeks a more holistic perspective on cuisine by comparing two European societies, Britain and France, with a non-Western society undergoing many of the same changes, Japan. The final chapter also takes a comparative view of the role of the state in mediating eighteenth-century social stress arising from population growth and agricultural innovation.

The pace of social and dietary change accelerated during the nineteenth century. Part II opens with a chapter examining the industrialization of provisioning systems. New technologies greatly increased food supplies by radically separating production from consumption, changing the way foods taste and even the definitions of wholesomeness. Chapter 7 examines the rise of nationalism, which transformed politics in an equally dramatic fashion in Europe and the Americas. The aristocratic privileges of court cuisine fit poorly with notions of popular sovereignty, and new elites fostered national cuisines as a way of making abstract political doctrines comprehensible in the everyday lives of citizens. By contrast, for Asians and Africans, industrialization and nationalism offered not greater freedom and prosperity but rather new forms of imperial oppression. Yet although European powers sought to transform colonial agriculture to their own advantage, Chapter 8 shows how their subjects preserved considerable cultural autonomy and even influenced metropolitan eating habits. Proletarian migrants, the focus of Chapter 9, sought to bridge these worlds of privilege and subordination by bringing their traditional cultures to industrial countries. In doing so, they transformed the cuisines of both their old homelands and their adopted nations.

The continued spread of culinary industrialization and globalization in the twentieth century forms the subject of Part III. The twin forces of industry and nationalism culminated in global wars of previously unknown magnitude, undermining the West's newly won food security. Two chapters examine the new politics of food, Chapter 10 focusing on Western Europe, and Chapter 11 on developing nations. The return of peace brought renewed prosperity, but continued industrial rationalization left people even more anxious about the safety of their foods, another theme running through this section. These contradictions were likewise magnified as the food industry spread to new areas of the world. Modern agriculture increased overall production in former colonies but at the same time exacerbated inequalities in conflict-ridden societies. Moreover, some came to fear that a handful of multinational corporations would obliterate local cultures, replacing traditional food habits with a bland and unhealthy "McDiet." Nevertheless, there were also rising challenges to Western cultural hegemony, as the final chapter shows. Thus, the future of global provisioning systems and eating habits remains uncertain at the start of the third millennium.

One conclusion that emerges from this narrative is the historical nature of globalization. The very term may seem vague and menacing, but if "globalization" is taken to mean the intensification of cultural and trade connections, then clearly it has been ongoing for centuries, at least in culinary forms. Although contemporary novelties such as fast food and fusion cuisine may appear unprecedented, they too represent a continuation of historical trends. Examining earlier forms of cultural contact and innovation can therefore help to evaluate claims about present-day globalization. Understanding the historical reception of new foods provides a key to responding to the loss of diversity through industrial standardization. Moreover, previous experiences with imperial conquest or global migration can inform both public policy and personal initiative.

Continuities notwithstanding, appreciating historical change is equally important. Modern agriculture really has created unprecedented abundance, at least in the West, where citizens can scarcely imagine the meaning of food in societies plagued by famine. Social relationships centering on food are likewise changing as national cuisines subsume local specialties and as individual choice multiplies at the expense of family unity. Whether communities based on shared manufactured consumer preferences – the Pepsi Generation, for example – can provide the emotional satisfaction of more traditional social ties seems doubtful.

# Chapter 1

# The first world cuisine

"Civilization" is a product of agriculture, and while farming societies have not always been considered "civilized," nomads who fed themselves by hunting, gathering, or herding have invariably been dismissed as "barbarians" by their sedentary neighbors. The transition from hunting and gathering to agriculture took place first in the Near East, where a wealth of natural grasses provided the raw materials for plant domestication. The retreat of the last Ice Age, about 10,000 BCE, encouraged new strategies for accumulating food, and over time humans transformed wild species into more useful grains such as barley, oats, and wheat through an unconscious process of selecting favorable plants and encouraging their propagation. As food sources became more dependable, nomadic bands settled into agricultural villages at Jericho and Çatal Hüyük (in modern-day Turkey) by 8000 BCE. Early agriculturalists also domesticated fruits, nuts, and pulses. The favorable natural resources of the River Nile in Egypt and the Tigris and Euphrates rivers in Mesopotamia yielded agricultural surpluses, facilitating the development of complex societies in which unequal access to food helped to define hierarchies. This social differentiation in archaic states, about 2000 BCE, also led to the patriarchal subordination of women, an ironic twist given the crucial role of female gatherers in plant domestication.

Pastoral traditions arose simultaneously with agriculture in the Near East. Although dogs had hunted together with humans for thousands of years, the domestication of sheep, about 9000 BCE, provided the first herd animals. Cattle and goats were domesticated later, and spread through much of the Middle East and North Africa. The use of dairy products began around 6000 BCE, and usually involved some form of processing to make cheese, yogurt, and butter, rather than the consumption of raw milk. Livestock also contributed to agriculture by drawing plows and providing fertilizer, but the competition between pasture and farmland led to cultural differentiation between nomadic herders and sedentary farmers. Pigs became the preferred source of meat in cities because they reproduced quickly and ate garbage. Pastoral peoples such as the Hebrews considered them to be filthy animals unfit for human consumption.

The social functions of food, constructing hierarchies and differentiating between peoples, form the subject of this chapter. It examines three civilizations, two of the classical world, and one of the post-classical. The empires of China and Rome both developed sophisticated agriculture and considered the preparation of food as a mark of their civilized status, distinct from barbarian outsiders. By contrast, Islam drew on both agricultural and pastoral traditions to form a multiethnic society that spanned three continents. The banquets of Baghdad were arguably the site of the first world cuisine, but elite foods of Rome and China likewise depended on exotic ingredients brought from distant lands.

## Chinese cuisine

Although rice has become the indispensable staple of modern Asia, historical Chinese civilization emerged in the arid north, a region unfit for rice cultivation. People settled into agricultural villages in the Yellow River valley as early as 7000 BCE, growing the nutritious grain millet. Rice domestication probably took place in a number of hearths, stretching from South-east Asia to the Yangtze River valley, which eventually became the Chinese agricultural heartland. The seemingly more primitive nomadic lifestyle actually developed later, about 2000 BCE, when Turkic peoples brought horseback riding skills to the western steppe. Chinese cuisine thus developed from earliest times with the recognition of regional differences.

The Chinese state acknowledged this agrarian basis, and the ancient classics ranked food as the first of eight concerns of government. According to legend, the founder of the Shang dynasty (c. 1766–1122 BCE) appointed his cook Yi Yin to be prime minister, and the cooking cauldron served as the prime symbol of government. Emperors conducted elaborate ritual sacrifices to propitiate the gods and ancestors, thereby ensuring good harvests. After deposing the Shang, the Western Zhou dynasty (c. 1040–771 BCE) asserted its legitimacy to rule, the Mandate of Heaven, by claiming descent from the millet god.

The regulation of food remained a central concern with the rise of Chinese social philosophy during the Eastern Zhou dynasty (770–256 BCE). Confucius (551–479 BCE), who emphasized gentlemanly conduct and strict observance of social hierarchies, extended this decorum to the finest details of food preparation. The *Analects* described his fastidious behavior when dining: "Undercooked foods he does not eat, and foods served at improper times he does not eat. Meat that is improperly carved, he does not eat, and if he does not obtain the proper sauce, he will not eat." Conflating personal behavior with the body politic, Confucius likened a well-planned meal to a well-governed state. Mencius (372–289 BCE) similarly averred that the primary duty of a ruler was to ensure that his subjects were properly fed. Even the draconian Legalist school, which opposed Confucian thought on most subjects, agreed that productive agriculture was essential for the well-being of the state.

A concern with balance and form had already infused Chinese cooking methods and eating rituals by the Eastern Zhou. The first step in preparing a proper meal lay in balancing staple grains with condiments such as meat and vegetables. Of necessity, the poor ate large bowls of rice or millet porridge, supplemented by soybeans, but the food canons (dietary guides) advised the wealthy likewise to avoid excessive quantities of rich foods. Confucius again set the example: "Though there is plenty of meat, he will not allow it to overcome the vitalizing power of the rice." Patterns of combining flavors and chopping ingredients, which are still distinctive characteristics of modern Chinese cuisine, had also been established; indeed, the cook's art of balancing the five flavors (salty, bitter, sweet, sour, and piquant) came to mirror the cosmological balance of five elements (earth, wood, fire, water, and metal).

Cuisine likewise contributed to the formation of social hierarchies. The *Rites of Zhou* assigned more than 2,200 attendants, over half of an idealized imperial household, to the preparation of food and drink. Other works set the proper number of meat and vegetable dishes according to rank (a high minister merited eight while a lower official got only six) and age (with more variety reserved for the elderly). All people were assumed to eat four bowls of grain daily. The classics also prescribed strict rules for etiquette, giving particular attention to the deference owed by people of lower rank to their superiors. Prepared for an elite audience, these texts denounced the boorish behavior of the lower classes, although commoners doubtless maintained their own standards for proper conduct.

The Chinese predilection for opulent banquets coexisted uneasily with philosophical teachings of simplicity and spiritual nourishment. The *Daodejing*, attributed to the sixth-century mystic Laozi, warned simply: "The five flavors confuse one's palate." Mozi (470–391 BCE) explicitly denounced elite gourmandizing: "There is no need of combining the five tastes extremely well or harmonizing the different sweet odours. And efforts should not be made to procure rare delicacies from far countries."

A system of humoral medicine ultimately arose from this tension between luxury and simplicity. Applying the Daoist concept of yin and yang to foods, Chinese physicians advised patients to maintain good health by balancing "hot" and "cold" foods. These qualities indicated not temperature but their effects on the body: for instance, meat, ginger, and fried foods were "heating"; by contrast, cabbage, shellfish, and boiled foods were "cooling." A person with a fever should eat cooling foods, while a cold sufferer needed heating foods. Grains such as rice and millet were considered neutral. This system was formalized only in the fifth century CE after the arrival of Buddhism, and disagreements remained as to the exact nature of particular foods.

Centuries of stability under the Han dynasty (206 BCE–220 CE) allowed an agricultural revolution. Innovation had begun already in the Eastern Zhou dynasty with the forging of iron plows, and Han officials produced elaborate agricultural manuals and maintained state granaries to prevent famine. New cooking methods also contributed to productivity. Wheat, an inferior grain for making porridge, spread widely after the invention of noodles. Intensive agriculture tripled China's population to 60 million people, according to a census of 2 CE, but at the expense of more concentrated land holdings. Despite social welfare policies, the plight of peasants inspired numerous rebellions. Emperor Wang Mang (ruled 9–23 CE) attempted a program of land distribution, but was overthrown and killed.

Chinese agriculturalists also used cooking as a standard of civilization to distinguish themselves from the nomads living beyond the Great Wall. Savage tribes supposedly ate raw meat or did not eat grain, violating rules of civilized dining. Ethnic Chinese scrupulously avoided the milk and cheese consumed by pastoral barbarians, although by the Northern and Southern dynasties (317–589 CE), after numerous foreign invasions, dairy products had become accepted, at least among northern Chinese. Cooking displayed a marked regionalism as northerners looked with suspicion on the strange aquatic creatures, local produce, and spices of the south. Notwithstanding the Chinese self-image as the "Middle Kingdom," cultural contact was essential for the rise of its civilization, starting with contact between the Yellow and Yangtze River regions. This exchange of food products, as well as the construction of social identities in opposition to nomadic outsiders, also marked another great empire of the ancient world, Rome.

## Food in the classical Mediterranean

Unlike the Chinese, the Romans marched out on the road to empire as uncouth conquerors of a civilized Mediterranean world. The Etruscan kings who ruled Rome until the founding of the republic in 509 BCE were renowned for abundant agriculture and lavish banquets. Egypt, although past its prime, remained the paragon of civilization with the perpetually fertile Nile and already-ancient pyramids. The Greeks and the Phoenicians had meanwhile taken the initiative in establishing colonies and planting wheat, olives, and grapes throughout the Mediterranean and Black Sea basins. Merchants from these far-flung trade empires conducted a lucrative commerce in grain, oil, and wine, as well as such luxury goods as honey, spices, and *garum*, a pungent sauce made of fermented fish and aromatic herbs. The majority of people made a living by farming, but even the most self-sufficient peasants bought and sold goods through markets.

Everyday foods of the Roman Republic reflected the stoic frugality of the citizen–soldier cultivating a small plot of land. A simple porridge of emmer wheat, supplemented by protein-rich broad beans, comprised the bulk of the diet. Cabbages, greens, and other vegetables added variety to meals, and even urban dwellers maintained kitchen gardens. Produce was generally eaten raw as salads with plenty of olive oil, contrary to the Chinese practice of cooking everything. Strictly speaking, the Romans believed that the sun "cooked" vegetables, unlike truly raw meat. With sparse grass and fodder, even the rich ate little animal protein, and that was generally pork rather than fish, as the Greeks preferred, or beef. Wine was the universal drink, although quality varied greatly according to social class. Legionnaires on campaign ate meat as well as porridges or flat breads and drank watered vinegar.

Romans set aside these frugal everyday habits for civic banquets, which played an important role in political, social, and religious life. By definition, a banquet involved the consumption of sacrificial meat, fed directly to participants in religious celebrations or purchased afterward at market. In either case, the wealthy enjoyed the lion's share. While ostensibly a gathering of equals, the *convivium*, or communal dinner, reflected social and political hierarchies. Members of the patrician class entertained plebeian clients to ensure their votes, although senators frowned on the practice of offering free dinners for the masses as an abuse of the patron–client system. Plebeians also shared in this sociability by forming dining and funeral societies to distribute the costs.

Greco-Roman attitudes toward the state and the marketplace differed sharply from the Chinese preoccupation with public welfare. Democratic and republican ideals of self-reliant farmer–soldiers precluded the state from feeding the people directly, even in times of hunger. At most, private individuals expressed civic concern as benefactors (*euergetes*) for the poor. By the second century BCE, large landed estates (*latifundia*) worked by slaves had replaced the independent farmers who traditionally manned the legions. The brothers Marcus and Gaius Gracchus attempted to restore the social balance through land distribution beginning in 133 BCE, but they suffered the same fate as the Chinese reformer Wang Mang. Offering bread and circuses became an effective strategy for ambitious politicians like Julius Caesar. After the fall of the republic, the Emperor Augustus (ruled 28 BCE–14 CE) bureaucratized the food supply for the imperial capital, importing grain from Egypt to keep Rome's million inhabitants quiescent. Consumers elsewhere still depended on markets and the occasional charity of landowners.

Nostalgic Roman commentators blamed the corruption of republican virtue on Greek decadence. The satirist Plautus (254–184 BCE) dated the arrival of the first cook in Rome to the year 187, and indeed within half a century, Greek bread had begun to replace the traditional porridge. Eastward expansion also brought Rome in contact with the spice trade; a series of sumptuary laws followed, but to little effect. A cookbook attributed to Apicius documents the extravagant haute cuisine of the empire. Petronius's *Satyricon* described the vulgar feast of a *nouveau riche* former slave, Trimalchio, who berated a cook during one banquet for having served a whole pig without gutting it first. When the hapless fellow slashed the belly, the "slits widened out under the pressure from inside, and suddenly out poured, not the pig's bowels and guts, but link upon link of tumbling sausage and blood puddings." Moralists doubtless exaggerated the "Roman incidents" of purging, but the Greeks at least provided physicians to treat the effects of overeating. They advised diets balancing the four humors – blood, phlegm, and yellow and black bile – a system that also influenced Muslim and perhaps Chinese beliefs by way of the Hellenistic world.

Culinary definitions of civilization were therefore more problematic in Rome than in China. The consumption of bread and wine distinguished the Romans from the barbarians who ate excessive quantities of meat – perhaps even raw in the case of the Huns – and drank ale. But at the same time, the Romans sought to distance themselves from Greek excesses by imagining a rustic past. Even these distinctions blurred over time, as greater numbers of Germanic people settled within the empire. The newcomers adopted Roman habits such as a taste for wine but retained their pastoral economy, and eventually public handouts included meat, as did even slave rations. Such largesse was possible because land that had come under the plow at the height of Roman influence reverted to forest and pasture as the empire retreated. Although the collapse of the Han dynasty entailed a similar population decline, ethnic Chinese eventually absorbed the foreign invaders and restored imperial rule. Contradictions within Roman identity, exemplified by the Janus-faced attitude toward food, may have contributed to the Western Empire's inability to do likewise. Mediterranean eating habits continued to change as new civilizations arose in the post-classical era.

## Multiethnic eating in the Muslim world

Before founding the religion of Islam around 610 CE, the Prophet Muhammad led camel caravans across the Arabian Peninsula, thus bridging the nomadic lifestyle of the desert and the settled agricultural villages of oases and the coast. Islam likewise synthesized diverse cultural traditions into a new civilization. Muslim armies struck out under the second caliph, Umar ibn Abd al-Khattāb (ruled 634–644), and subjugated large parts of the Sasanid and Byzantine empires, thereby inheriting Persian and Greek cultural traditions. Within a century, Muslim rule extended from Spain across North Africa and the Middle East to India, offering access to ingredients and cooking methods from three continents and establishing the basis for a cuisine that spanned the known world.

The unified government of the caliphate encouraged widespread trade and migration, introducing Asian food crops to the west. Islam honored the merchant profession, and Arab traders soon dominated Indian Ocean shipping routes. *The Thousand and One Nights* described the wealth of produce available to Baghdad shoppers: "Syrian apples and Othmani quinces, Omani peaches, cucumbers from the Nile, Egyptian lemons and Sultani citrons." Low taxes, predominantly free labor, and the opportunity to own land enticed farmers from Persia and India to migrate westward, bringing with them sophisticated irrigation techniques and tropical Asian crops including rice, sugar, hard wheat, citrus fruits, bananas, mangoes, spinach, artichokes, and eggplants. Some plants of African origin such as watermelon and sorghum even made a roundabout voyage from the Swahili Coast to India, where they were improved, before returning to Africa and Europe. On pilgrimage to Mecca, the Spanish Muslim Ibn Jubayr described watermelons that tasted "like sugar-candy or purest honey" – a far cry from the bitter wild melons of Africa.

Despite this massive movement of people and plants, regional cuisines remained distinctive. The dairy and date-based diet of Bedouin shepherds, little changed since pre-Islamic times, contrasted with the lavish roast meats, rice pilafs, and sweet and savory combinations of Persian court cuisine. Cooks from Moorish Spain to Palestine specialized in fresh Mediterranean seafood, while others in the Middle East had access to only a limited variety of dried fish. Couscous, tiny steamed pasta made of sorghum and later hard wheat, spread slowly from Morocco and probably arrived in Syria and Iraq about the thirteenth century. By contrast, sweetmeats and pastries became ubiquitous throughout the Muslim world with the diffusion of sugar cane.

Islamic dietary laws imposed some continuity on these diverse regional cuisines. Pork was forbidden to Muslims, making mutton the favorite meat. Both Arab and Jewish butchers performed ritualized slaughter, draining the meat of all blood. The Qur'an also banned alcohol, which was eventually replaced by coffee. Muslims fasted for the month of Ramadan, neither eating nor drinking during the long, hot days, as opposed to Catholics, who abstained from meat during Lent. Although common to all societies, hospitality and charity had particularly deep roots in the harsh Arabian Desert, and the *zakāt* or tithe for the poor ranked among the five pillars of Islam. The generosity of such caliphs as Harun al-Rashid (ruled 786–809) expressed personal charity rather than the organized welfare policy of China, but this religious requirement imposed a stronger sense of responsibility than did the civic duty of classical Rome.

Handouts to the poor notwithstanding, the extravagant cuisine of the Abassid caliphate (750–1258) challenged the ethic of equality within the Muslim community. The ninth-century *Kitāb al-Bukhalā* (Book of Misers) berated Arabs for eating "Persian food, the food of Chosores, the flesh of the wheat in the saliva of the bee and the purest clarified butter . . . . Ibn al-Khattāb would not have approved." This reference to the spartan second caliph rebuked the contemporary Baghdad court for having been corrupted by Persian luxuries. The hand of fate, omnipresent in Arab literature, could also punish those distracted by delicate foods. Moroccan traveler Ibn Battūta related a tale worthy of *The Thousand and One Nights* about a theologian, Jalāl ad-Dīn, who was tempted by a sweetmeat vendor. "The shaykh left his lesson to follow him and disappeared for some years. Then he came back, but with a disordered mind, speaking nothing but Persian verses which no one could understand."

Cooks beyond the world of Islam also looked for inspiration to the cosmopolitan banquets of the caliphs. Medieval Christians had access to these recipes not so much from the Crusades as from Muslim-occupied areas of Spain and Sicily. In Italy, macaroni made of hard wheat had appeared by the thirteenth century, and two hundred years later, rice cultivation spread to the north, where cooks still make a porridge-like risotto. Scholars have traced connections between the sophisticated use of spices in Arabic cookbooks and European works of the late Middle Ages, although similar recipes in Apicius make it difficult to prove a direct influence. African cooks likewise benefited from the introduction of new ingredients and cooking techniques. The diffusion of crops tended to run westward, with fewer gains for Asia; nevertheless, the Sultanate of Delhi (1206–1526) left a deep imprint on North Indian cooking. Muslim recipes also appeared in Chinese domestic manuals of the Song dynasty (960–1279), but their influence was overshadowed by an indigenous culinary revolution resulting from improved strains of Vietnamese rice and an emerging market economy. As the Chinese population surpassed 100 million in the twelfth century, Hangzhou restaurants boasted as diverse a cuisine as that of the Baghdad court.

With their identity firmly rooted in submission to God, Muslims needed few stereotypes about barbaric foods to differentiate themselves from nonbelievers. Arab merchants and pilgrims traveled widely and expressed an intense curiosity about the customs and foods of the people they encountered. Their tolerance of "peoples of the book," including Christians, Jews, and later Hindus and Buddhists as well, likewise helped establish the most universal cuisine of the post-classical world.

## Conclusion

Tensions between pastoral and agricultural societies reflected ecological, health, and moral concerns. A basic competition for land between plow and pasture translated into cultural ideals, as farmers denounced the vagabond life of nomads, who in turn shunned the monotony of an enclosed field. The medical condition of lactose intolerance made milk seem disgusting to adult Chinese, although butter, cheese, and yogurt were widely consumed in India and the Mediterranean world. Even without the meat available to nomadic bands, agrarian societies balanced staple grains with soybeans, broad beans, and other protein-rich legumes. Vegetarian peasant cuisines were basically sound, but subclinical levels of malnutrition were widespread in the ancient world, as in contemporary developing societies.

The three civilizations examined in this chapter all created elaborate cuisines that reinforced social hierarchies and separated "cultured" insiders from "barbaric" foreigners. Nevertheless, the degree of dietary restrictions for moral or health reasons varied widely; Chinese and Romans held fewer taboos than their Hindu and Jewish neighbors. All societies depended on outsiders for some foods, particularly spices and other luxuries, which formed an important source of long-distance trade. Just as access to food differed by social status, the preparation of food reinforced gender inequalities. Male chefs created elaborate court cuisines and male priests generally fed the gods, while women were relegated to everyday cooking. Cultural patterns inherited from stable agrarian societies proved to be extremely persistent even as the early modern era initiated radical transformations in the production and consumption of food.

## Further reading

On early agriculture, Kenneth F. Kiple and Kriemhild Coneè Kiple (eds), *The Cambridge World History of Food*, 2 vols. (Cambridge: Cambridge University Press, 2000). For China, K. C. Chang (ed.), *Food in Chinese Culture* (New Haven, CT: Yale University Press, 1977); E. N. Anderson, *The Food of China* (New Haven, CT: Yale University Press, 1988); David Knechtges, "A Literary Feast: Food in Early Chinese Literature," *Journal of the American Oriental Society* 106(1) (1986): 49–63. On Mediterranean civilizations, Jean-Louis Flandrin and Massimo Montanari (eds), *Food: A Culinary History*, trans. Albert Sonnenfeld (New York: Columbia University Press, 1999); Peter Garnsey, *Food and Society in Classical Antiquity* (Cambridge: Cambridge University Press, 1999); and Emily Gowers, *The Loaded Table: Representations of Food in Roman Literature* (Oxford: Clarendon Press, 1993). On Islam, Maxime Rodinson, A. J. Arberry, and Charles Perry, *Medieval Arab Cookery* (Devon: Prospect Books, 2001); and Andrew M. Watson, *Agricultural Innovation in the Early Islamic World: The Diffusion of Crops and Farming Techniques, 700–1100* (Cambridge: Cambridge University Press, 1983).

# Part I

# The ingredients of change

Agrarian economies of the pre-modern era were powered primarily by human and animal labor and consequently moved with the long-term rhythms of population growth and decline. Agricultural innovations, ranging from rice mills invented in the Han Dynasty to new crops introduced by Muslim traders, therefore had greater economic significance than did long-distance trade in commodities such as spices, which were limited to the wealthy. The incipient globalization of food production during the early modern era stimulated widespread demographic and economic expansion while also contributing to profound social change.

European powers, the leading beneficiaries of this change, greatly increased their global political influence. During the post-classical era, medieval Europe had existed on the periphery of trade networks centered on the Indian Ocean. Portuguese and Dutch cannon soon won control of the seaways, even as Spanish conquistadors seized a vast land empire in the Americas. Nevertheless, limits remained on European hegemony in the early modern era. Maritime nations acquired only small trading outposts in Asia and Africa, where they operated with the tolerance of local potentates, and non-Western merchants skillfully redirected much of the spice trade beyond their reach. Despite the devastating consequences of new diseases, Native American subjects also reached accommodations with colonial rulers to preserve much of their cultural autonomy, particularly in the foods they consumed.

The rise of the tropical plantation system was another significant effect of European expansion. Sugar plantations arose in the Caribbean and Brazil, using, first, Native American labor, and when they succumbed to disease and overwork, imported African slaves filled the gap. The trans-Atlantic trade ultimately uprooted more than 10 million people from the sixteenth to the nineteenth centuries. Such a drain on Africa's population was made possible by the introduction of high-yielding food crops from the Americas, although increased productivity did little to alleviate the social and economic dislocations caused by the trade in human lives. Profits from the plantation system naturally accrued to the European colonial powers, as sugar became one of the first modern, global commodities. In the form of rum, it helped finance

the purchase of African slaves, while as molasses it fueled their arduous plantation labor. More refined sugar crystals, together with coffee, tea, and chocolate,
which were also produced in tropical plantations, allowed an unprecedented
form of mass consumption among the working classes of Europe. The nutritional
value of these commodities was low, but they provided a cheap source of energy
that contributed to European industrialization.

The early modern period was also a time of political consolidation in which
kings and emperors sought to centralize authority at the expense of traditional
rivals. Feudalism had provided the European aristocracy with great autonomy,
yet internal conflicts between kings and nobles could have grave consequences
in a time of increasing rivalries between states, beginning with the sixteenth-
century wars of religion and culminating in eighteenth-century dynastic
struggles. As monarchs claimed absolute power, many nobles turned to cultural
pursuits, including cooking, as a way to distinguish themselves from the rising
middle classes. Nevertheless, such political developments proceeded unevenly,
with absolutism reaching a pinnacle in eighteenth-century France and Russia
while British nobles successfully limited the power of the monarchy. In East
Asia, new dynasties likewise succeeded in centralizing authority, although
the Ottomans in the Middle East and the Mughals of India declined under the
influence of centrifugal forces.

Even as monarchs gradually triumphed over their former rivals, they confronted new challenges from the rising middle classes. In Europe and the
Americas, the growth of commercial capitalism, including the spice and sugar
trade, allowed merchants and professionals to accumulate great wealth. Denied
access to courtly society, they sought new forums to demonstrate cultural
accomplishments and voice political aspirations. Coffeehouses became an
important public space in which these middling sorts asserted their distinction
from both the aristocracy and the working classes. In Asia, by contrast, fear
of the disruptive effects of concentrated wealth led to firmer restrictions on
merchants' political activities.

Even in the most traditional societies, population growth and economic
expansion proved deeply unsettling. One symptom of this eighteenth-century
transformation was a global wave of food riots, even as the diffusion of crops
and agricultural technologies provided greater overall food security. Responses
to social disruptions varied widely. China's bureaucratic elite, versed in the
doctrines of Confucian responsibility, mobilized tremendous resources to feed
a rapidly growing population. States lacking strong central authority, such as
the Ottoman Empire, declined further. In Europe, the dilemma of urban
provisioning became the crux of alternative approaches to political modernity.
British elites acquired a deep faith in the ability of markets to distribute food
most efficiently and therefore pursued *laissez-faire* policies even in the face
of terrible famines. The French experience with food riots instilled quite a
different attitude toward the balance of public and private interests, and these
rival interpretations helped shape the development of industrial capitalism.

# Chapter 2

# The Columbian Exchange

Columbus's 1492 voyage in search of a western passage to the Spice Islands began a fundamental transformation in the eating habits of all humans. The immediate biological and environmental consequences of contact between Europe and the Americas were dramatic, as exposure to Old World diseases killed more than 80 percent of the New World population within a hundred years. Aided by this unintentional germ warfare, Spanish conquistadors quickly subdued the vast Aztec, Maya, and Inca empires. European plants and animals flourished in the fields left open by demographic decline, transforming the ecology of the Americas, but the Spaniards succeeded only partially in their goal of establishing colonial replicas of their homeland. Surviving natives intermarried with European colonists and with African slaves, creating new ethnic blends. Highly productive food crops domesticated in the New World not only persisted as essential staples for both natives and newcomers alike, they were also carried back across the Atlantic and launched a demographic revolution in the Old World, helping set the stage for modern population growth.

Yet these changes were far from uniform. Peasants in China, Africa, and the Middle East began planting American staples as soon as they arrived in the sixteenth century, but in Europe and India these crops were largely ignored for hundreds of years. Fruits and vegetables likewise spread in an irregular fashion, and Europeans who had pioneered the new trade routes to America were the least likely to adopt the crops they had discovered. The circuitous routes by which new plants traveled also led to popular uncertainty about their origins.

Material and cultural factors combined to determine the acceptance of new foods. Ecology had a role, for plants grew best in environments similar to those in which they had been domesticated. Tropical crops could not resist freezing temperatures, but changes in altitude and microclimates allowed ecological flexibility. Productivity and compatibility with existing rotations also mattered to farmers considering new crops. Cooks likewise had their say, for an unfamiliar plant, however prolific, was unlikely to gain favor if it could not be prepared in a tasty and appealing fashion. Although a global process, the Columbian Exchange was nevertheless negotiated at the local level.

## Mexico

The absence of domesticated animals, apart from turkeys and small dogs, distinguished the civilizations of Mesoamerica from other classical empires. Native Americans excelled at foraging for protein but still depended overwhelmingly on their staple grain, maize. Human labor provided the main source of energy, as women ground maize by hand while men carried heavy loads on their backs. The introduction of livestock by Spanish conquistadors therefore had the potential for improving livelihoods but also posed great environmental dangers for indigenous farmers unaccustomed to pastoral herds.

The Mesoamerican maize complex provided the foundation for a basically vegetarian diet. The grain supplied carbohydrates and up to 80 percent of total calories while beans added protein; complementary amino acids magnified the nutritional value of the pair by forming a complete protein when eaten together. Chiles, squash, tomatoes, and avocadoes offered vitamins, minerals, and interesting flavors. Native Americans supplemented this vegetarian cuisine by consuming virtually all available animal protein: deer, ducks, rabbits, seafood, and even rodents, insects, and lake algae.

Indigenous techniques for preparing maize tortillas were extremely labor-intensive. Mesoamerican women first simmered the kernels in a mineral solution, which loosened the indigestible husk and released niacin, a vitamin necessary to avoid the disease pellagra. The next step involved hand-grinding the wet dough, called *nixtamal*, while kneeling painfully over a grinding stone. Women then patted the smooth dough into thin, round tortillas and cooked them briefly on an earthenware griddle. Because tortillas quickly went stale and *nixtamal* fermented overnight, women had to rise hours before dawn to cook for men going to work in the fields. Midwives warned newborn girls: "Thou wilt become fatigued, thou wilt become tired; thou art to provide water, to grind maize, to drudge." The subjugation of the grinding stone inspired a particularly oppressive version of patriarchy in Mesoamerica.

With limited supplies, social hierarchies governed food distribution. Well-fed nobles stood some ten centimeters taller than commoners in the classical Maya city of Tikal (fourth–eighth centuries CE). A terrible famine in the year One Rabbit (1454), in the early stages of Aztec imperial expansion, focused attention on food supplies for the island capital of Tenochtitlan. At the time, Moctezuma the Elder used canoes to distribute maize to starving people, and in later years, the Great Feast of the Lords recalled this imperial beneficence through ceremonial handouts of tamales (maize dumplings) from canoes. The Aztec Empire demanded tribute of food and other goods from subject peoples, especially in the productive raised fields of Lake Chalco-Xochimilco. Among the warrior elite, civic and religious banquets assumed a competitive nature, with each host attempting to serve the finest chile pepper stews, tamales, and hot chocolate. Spanish conquistadors spoke with awe about the hundreds of lavish dishes served daily to Moctezuma the Younger (ruled 1502–1520).

Nevertheless, mutual disgust marked the culinary encounter between Spaniards and Native Americans. Moctezuma's emissaries reported that European bread tasted "like dried maize stalks," while Bernal Díaz del Castillo complained of the "misery of maize cakes" that served as rations during the conquest. Natives ranked pork fat among the tortures brought by the Spaniards, who were equally disgusted by the indigenous consumption of rodents and insects, dubbed *"animalitos."* Catholic missionaries attempted to propagate wheat in order to replace maize gods with the Holy Eucharist, but peasants found the Europe grain unproductive, expensive to grow, and prone to disease, although some entrepreneurial natives cultivated it for sale to urban Hispanic markets. As a result, wheat bread and maize tortillas became status markers within the racial hierarchy called the system of castes.

Even more devastating was the invasion of European livestock, as cattle and sheep reproduced at exponential rates and overran the countryside. The simultaneous growth of herds and collapse of human population due to disease made it appear as if the livestock were eating the natives. For a few decades in the mid-sixteenth century, meat sold for a pittance in Mexico City, but with uncontrolled grazing, herbivores soon exceeded the carrying capacity of the land, exposing the soil to erosion and rendering it unfit for farming or herding. In just a few decades, sheep turned the fertile Mezquital Valley into a barren desert, and by the end of the century, meat was again scarce in colonial markets.

Devastation and disgust notwithstanding, culinary fusion had already begun in sixteenth-century Mesoamerica. Although retaining their staple maize, native cooks learned to whip pork fat into tamales, giving the cakes a lighter texture and richer flavor. Spanish settlers meanwhile acquired a taste for beans and chile peppers, even while paying high prices for familiar wheat bread. This process of cultural blending was repeated in South America as well.

## Peru

The Andes Mountains rise like some Brobdingnagian terraced field, with separate ecological niches providing a wealth of different foodstuffs. Abundant supplies of fish and shellfish supported complex societies as early as 2500 BCE in the otherwise desert climate on the Pacific coast, where strong currents bring fog but no rain. Ascending the slopes into temperate highland valleys, the Mesoamerican maize complex coexisted with the Andean grain, quinoa. Farther up, in the cold, rainy zone above the treeline, human settlements depended on potatoes and other root crops such as *oca* and *ulloco*. At the highest elevations grazed llamas, domesticated camelids used to carry trade goods up and down the mountains, as well as smaller alpacas, which provided fine wool.

Coca leaves, cultivated along the eastern slopes, were chewed as a stimulant by people living in the highlands. The exchange of food and other goods between such diverse climates became a central aspect of the diets and lives of Andean peoples.

To transport food such great distances without spoiling, Andean cooking relied heavily on methods for preservation. Highland farmers exposed potatoes to frost and sun to make freeze-dried *chuño*. Shepherds dried llama meat into *charqui* (hence the English word "jerky") and cooked blood into gruel similar to European black puddings. Meanwhile, salted and sun-dried fish arrived from the coastal lowlands. Guinea pigs, another important source of animal protein, reproduced so quickly as to obviate the need for preservation; they were simply boiled or roasted. Andean women likewise boiled and toasted maize. Without the need for laborious daily maize grinding, women worked as shepherds and farmers, planting and harvesting potatoes while men turned the soil with footplows, and as a result, they had greater social equality than in Mexico.

The Inca Empire (1438–1532) built a highly productive economy on Andean traditions of reciprocity, whereby leaders organized labor and redistributed wealth for the benefit of the entire community. Having conquered a vast realm, stretching 3,000 kilometers from present-day Ecuador to Chile, the Inca restructured these societies for maximum efficiency, for example, by resettling entire highland villages at lower elevations in order to increase the production of maize. The Inca not only uprooted communities but also dispersed them up and down the Andes Mountains, creating social "archipelagos" known as *ayllu*, in which kinfolk lived at different elevations and harvested seafood, maize, potatoes, and coca for exchange within these geographically extended families. *Ayllus* also had a responsibility for supplying labor tribute to herd llamas and to produce food, clothing, and other goods for the imperial government. The Inca maintained enormous granaries, both as military depots and as distribution centers, and kept careful records of food supplies using *quipus*, indigenous balance sheets that recorded numbers using a system of knots tied on strings. Local lords, called *kurakas*, served as intermediaries between the state and the people by allocating tribute duties and distributing food. The ideal of equality notwithstanding, nobles ate far more meat than commoners. According to early chronicles, Topa Inca (ruled 1471–1493) even ordered runners to carry "fresh fish from the sea, and as it was seventy or eighty leagues from the coast to Cuzco . . . they were brought alive and twitching."

Disease and brutality made the conquest of Peru as devastating as that of Mexico, but prior pastoral experience helped mitigate the environmental consequences of the Columbian Exchange. The rapacious Spaniards systematically looted Inca warehouses, seizing any treasure and selling off the foodstuffs. By the fall of 1539, less than a decade after their arrival, people were starving in Cuzco, despite the rapid population decline. Disease also decimated llamas, although from an indigenous source rather than a pathogen imported from Europe. Inca shepherds had carefully culled any animals infected with *caracha*, but after the breakdown of the native administration, this disease spread through the herds, killing two-thirds of the indigenous camelids. The conquistadors ordered Andean shepherds to tend cattle and sheep instead, a policy that at least helped protect indigenous farmers. Nevertheless, Spaniards often purposely turned livestock loose to damage indigenous fields and irrigation works in order to claim the land for their own uses, especially to grow wheat and sugar cane.

The development of food habits in post-conquest Mexico and Peru provides an interesting comparative study in cultural accommodation. Both colonies became productive centers for European agriculture, with diverse ecological niches supporting wheat, sugar cane, and livestock. Nevertheless, two other mainstays of the Mediterranean diet, olive oil and wine, flourished in Peru but not in Mexico. Favorable climates existed in both regions although unpredictable frosts frustrated early attempts at winemaking in Mexico. Nor does Spanish trade policy explain the differences because decrees establishing peninsular monopolies for these products came only after regional agriculture patterns had become fixed. Perhaps colonists in Mexico simply came to prefer the taste of substitutes – pork fat and hot chocolate – along with chiles and beans. Indigenous nobles in both colonies claimed status by adopting European foods, but commoners preferred their accustomed staples, maize and potatoes, and accepted imports at the margins of their diet; for example, *anticuchos* (grilled beef heart) became a street food of indigenous Peruvians in urban areas. Meanwhile, American crops had begun to transform the Old World.

## Return passages

In America, Columbus encountered foods that ultimately yielded far more benefits than the Asian spices he had originally sought, but Europeans proved curiously slow in exploiting those new culinary treasures. Instead of taking root in Iberian fields, these crops passed by way of Spanish and Portuguese merchants to the Middle East, Africa, and Asia. They gained European acceptance hundreds of years later. A number of factors helped determine the spread of new crops, including their productivity and fit within agricultural regimes, their ease of preparation and adaptability to culinary systems, and the cultural associations that they evoked.

Maize, the most versatile and productive plant domesticated in the Americas, illustrates the ambivalent reception of new crops. Columbus carried it back to Spain in 1493, but lacking the gluten to make leavened bread, it was prepared as porridge and considered to be a famine food at best. In 1597, John Gerard described it as "a more convenient food for swine than for men." By contrast, the American grain diffused rapidly in the Middle East, where porridges did not have such inferior status. Arriving in Lebanon and Syria by the 1520s, corn helped spur population growth under the Ottoman Emperor Süleyman the Magnificent (ruled 1520–1566). As a result, many Europeans referred to maize as the "Turkish" grain while in India it was known as "Mecca" corn. The Portuguese introduced it to West Africa, where it surpassed the productivity of millet and sorghum, although the latter was still more drought-resistant. From northern India, maize spread through inland Chinese provinces of Yunnan and Sichuan in the seventeenth century. The labor-intensive technique of making *nixtamal*, however, remained limited to Mesoamerica; Old World cooks prepared the new cultivar using familiar methods, either roasting it on the cob like a vegetable or else grinding it into flour for porridge or, in China, noodles.

Chile peppers likewise spread most rapidly in cuisines that already used spices liberally. Although colonists in New Spain quickly acquired a taste for chile sauces prepared by Native American cooks, western Europeans accustomed to powdered cinnamon, nutmeg, and pepper, hesitated to touch the hot plant, which burned the hands as well as the mouth. The principal staging point for the chile's invasion of the Old World was therefore India, where they were introduced by Portuguese traders and fit naturally into the complex spice blends, prepared as pastes and generically called "curry" by Europeans. Areas of Indian cultural influence such as Thailand quickly adopted the new condiments, and they were also carried overland on the Silk Road to Sichuan and Yunnan, Chinese regions now known for fiery dishes, as well as to Turkey and hence Hungary, where people became addicted to the chile powder, paprika. Chiles also spread widely through Africa as a complement to spices arriving from the Indian Ocean trade.

Social conditions influenced the diffusion of American crops, as can be seen by comparing the experience of China and India. Despite intensive agriculture, China's population had reached its ecological limits in the final years of the Ming dynasty (1368–1644). As famines struck, starving peasants eagerly adopted American foodstuffs, particularly the sweet potato, which provided multiple crops with a greater caloric yield even than rice, did not require laborious transplanting and paddy maintenance, and could be grown on otherwise marginal land. Whether baked, boiled, mashed, or ground into flour for noodles and porridge, sweet potatoes became a fixture of virtually every meal in South China. Maize and peanuts likewise complemented existing crop rotations, multiplying agricultural productivity. In India, by contrast, the Mughals ruled a more mobile society with considerable available land and relatively slow population growth. Farmers thus had little incentive to intensify production and largely ignored the American staples maize and potatoes until the nineteenth century.

European reluctance to adopt American crops begins to make sense when viewed from a broader perspective. Recurring bouts of plague left room for population growth until famines drove northern Europeans to adopt the potato, starting with Ireland in the seventeenth century and moving east through

France, Germany, and Russia in the eighteenth and nineteenth centuries. Maize likewise became a staple in southern Europe but without losing its initial association as an animal fodder. Even the tomato, which had arrived in Naples by the 1550s, did not appear in Italian cookbooks until the end of the seventeenth century, although peasants had no doubt eaten it sooner. Thus, the lethargy with which medieval Europeans adopted Muslim crops continued to characterize the early modern spread of American foodstuffs.

## Conclusion

Religious imperatives drove both Aztec and Inca imperial expansion, but the common belief in reciprocity took different forms in Middle and South America. The Inca, like the Chinese, emphasized the distribution of food as essential to good government, while the Aztec tribute system functioned primarily to supply food to the metropolis, as in imperial Rome, in addition to sacrificial victims for the maize gods. It is difficult to explain these differences considering material causes alone, but the labor-intensive production of maize tortillas does help account for the greater inequality of gender relations in Mesoamerica.

A broad view of material and cultural factors is likewise necessary to explain the uneven nature of the Columbian Exchange. Demographic pressure encouraged the adoption of new crops in Europe and Asia, while population declines helped spread livestock in the Americas. Landholding patterns and agricultural regimes also influenced the selection of new crops. Native Americans cultivated wheat only under Spanish compulsion because of the expense of heavy plows, grinding mills, and ovens. Disgust and fear also delayed the spread of both tomatoes and potatoes, which were considered potentially dangerous in Europe.

Although seeds often traveled independently of farmers, agricultural and culinary knowledge had an important role in the Columbian Exchange. Because Native American women, with their knowledge of *nixtamal*, did not travel to the Old World, populations that adopted maize as the staple grain were subject to the dietary deficiency disease pellagra. The limited inward migration to Europe during the early modern period may have slowed the diffusion of crops; indeed, American crops took hundreds of years to achieve their full demographic effect. By that time, Europeans had developed new systems of production and trade with profound historical consequences.

## Further reading

This chapter was inspired by Alfred W. Crosby, Jr., *The Columbian Exchange: Biological and Cultural Consequences of 1492* (Westport, CT: Greenwood Press, 1972). See also, Sophie Coe, *America's First Cuisines* (Austin, TX: University of Texas Press, 1994); John C. Super, *Food, Conquest, and Colonization in Sixteenth-Century Spanish America* (Albuquerque, NM: University of New Mexico Press, 1988); and Elinor G.

K. Melville, *A Plague of Sheep: Environmental Consequences of the Conquest of Mexico* (Cambridge: Cambridge University Press, 1997). On the diffusion of American foods, William Langer, "American Foods and Europe's Population Growth, 1750–1850," *Journal of Social History* 8(2) (Winter 1975): 51–66; Nelson Foster and Linda Cordell (eds), *Chiles to Chocolate: Food the Americas Gave the World* (Tucson, AZ: University of Arizona Press, 1992); Sucheta Mazumdar, "The Impact of New World Food Crops on the Diet and Economy of China and India, 1600–1900," in Raymond Grew (ed.), *Food in Global History* (Boulder, CO: Westview Press, 1999); and Arturo Warman, *Corn and Capitalism: How a Botanical Bastard Grew to Global Dominance*, trans. Nancy L. Westrate (Chapel Hill, NC: University of North Carolina Press, 2003).

# Chapter 3

# Sugar, spice, and blood

Spices pervaded the aristocratic cuisines of late medieval Europe, and cookbooks of the era specified quantities of pepper, clove, and nutmeg that appear outlandish to modern readers. While some might imagine that meat must have been thoroughly rotten to need such excessive condiments, spices were actually used for their social prestige, as an expensive import, and for dietary reasons, to balance "hot" and "cold" foods according to humoral medicine. Yet regardless of its origins, the spice trade launched mariners in search of a route to the Indies, thus beginning a process of imperial expansion that culminated with European hegemony over most of the world. The taste for spices proved ironically short-lived, declining by the seventeenth century, but overseas empires also supplied new foods with even greater demand. Sugar, in particular, became both a centerpiece of modern diets and the cause of suffering for millions of African slaves, transported to the Americas to work and die in tropical plantations.

Sugar and spice not only fueled Europe's drive to empire, they also contributed to the rise of capitalism. Although historians often date the beginnings of this modern economic system to nineteenth-century Britain, industrialization depended on sophisticated financial markets developed by earlier commercial enterprises. The Dutch United East India Company (*Vereenigde Oostindische Compagnie*, VOC), which dominated the spice trade, has been described as a multinational corporation with a sales office in Europe. Even the technological structures of industrial capitalism had parallels in seventeenth-century sugar plantations, which constituted veritable "factories in the fields," with mechanized production and a tightly organized workforce, albeit using coerced rather than free labor.

The rise of new trade routes and plantation systems also caused a fundamental shift in the economic balance of power, forging a new Atlantic system as the hub of global exchange. Until 1500, Europe had been peripheral to the Indian Ocean trade, receiving only a trickle of spices. Maritime empires gave European powers direct control over the riches of the East, even as the slave trade connected Africa and America to Europe through chains of forced migration and commercial exchange.

Although European empires controlled the broad outlines of this system, Muslim merchants and African slaves nevertheless found spaces for preserving their own autonomy. Asians clung tenaciously to a portion of the spice trade, for both commercial and culinary reasons. Moreover, Africans transplanted to the Americas many aspects of their traditional cultures, including their diverse cooking habits.

## Africa's many cuisines

The people of Sub-Saharan Africa overcame enormous ecological hurdles to accumulate agricultural surpluses and build great civilizations. Weather patterns confounded farmers with recurring droughts in the savanna and excessive rainfall in tropical forests. Clearing the soil for planting caused rapid erosion and also created breeding grounds for the *anopheles* mosquito, which carried malaria. Moreover, the tsetse fly spread sleeping sickness to both humans and livestock, making pastoralism difficult in a broad zone around the Equator. Even salt was precious, at times exchanging on par with gold in the trans-Saharan trade. Yet the precarious nature of the food supply bound people together. Migration linked different ethnic groups and encouraged cooperation between farmers and herders, while agricultural labor gave status within the family to women and even slaves.

By the post-classical era, the diffusion of foodstuffs through diverse climates had yielded a variety of connected yet distinct regional cuisines. The Sudan, between the Sahara and the equatorial rainforest, was the site of domestication for many important plants. West African varieties of rice yielded multiple paddy and upland harvests thanks to sophisticated earthworks built along the Niger and Senegal Rivers. A yam belt stretched across the woodland savanna from the modern Côte d'Ivoire to the Cameroon, an area that was also favorable for oil palms. Farther north, in the grasslands flanking the Sahara Desert, farmers cultivated millet and sorghum. Black-eyed peas, groundnuts, okra, greens, and baobab fruits supplemented diets in all these regions. In the cool highlands of Ethiopia, indigenous *teff* (a grain used for the broad flatbread, *ingera*), sesame, and coffee grew alongside wheat, barley, and chickpeas, which were introduced by way of the Red Sea.

Bantu and other migratory peoples carried both African domesticates and transplanted crops throughout the southern extension of the continent. The rich natural resources of the Great Lakes region attracted diverse peoples skilled in yam cultivation, cattle herding, and fishing; the merging of these traditions through trade, intermarriage, and cooperative hunting parties produced a distinctive cultural synthesis. Bananas, introduced from Asia, proved ideal for the equatorial rainforest, yielding ten times the caloric output of yams and requiring far less cleared land, hence limiting the spread of malaria. The resulting population growth revolutionized society in the Congo, leading to the rise of kingdoms by the fourteenth century. Mercantile cities on the

Swahili Coast imported spices and wheat for making curry and *chapati* bread as well as Chinese porcelain in exchange for slaves, gold, and ivory.

Livestock contributed significantly to African diets, and breeds such as dwarf shorthorn cattle were specially adapted to the tropical climate. Pastoralists often coexisted in a symbiotic relationship with more sedentary people, trading meat and dairy products for cultivated foods, and at times even tending livestock for farmers. The Fulani of West Africa practiced a form of transhumance, and during the dry season, when the danger from tsetse flies was low, they ran cattle down from the savanna into Mande rice fields, providing fertilizer for the next harvest. Among many agricultural societies as well, herding became a male perquisite, and cattle conferred social prestige.

Women gained status by cultivating the land and cooking. African agriculture depended on the hoe rather than the plow, which damaged the fragile soil. The basic kitchen utensil, a mortar and pestle, allowed women to mill rice and grains, to mash yams, and to prepare condiments. Cooks typically arranged a hearth of three stones, then boiled porridge and prepared relishes such as groundnut and okra soups or greens seasoned with palm oil and malaguetta peppers. Fermented alcoholic beverages often provided women with independent income. These brews varied regionally from millet beer in the savanna and sweet palm wine in woodland areas to Ethiopian honey wine and banana beer in the rainforest. Women even participated in those seemingly male activities of hunting and herding by trapping small animals, milking cattle, and tending other livestock.

Subsistence needs prompted local elites to maintain strict control over provisioning. Long-distance caravans traded staple grains, dried fish and meat, and kola nuts, which were chewed to quench thirst and stay hunger. Nevertheless, even in such great cities as Djenne and Mombasa, residents cultivated nearby fields for their own needs, and urban vendors often specialized in retailing prepared foods to visiting merchants. Village leaders gained legitimacy by distributing food through regular feasts painstakingly cooked by their wives. Slaves also contributed to the agricultural work and were considered valued members of the extended family, although of inferior status. Beginning in the fifteenth century, these social and political institutions were threatened by new participants in the slave trade, Portuguese merchants sailing around the African coast in search of a route to the Orient.

## Spice wars

Although endowed by geography with a natural monopoly, the spice trade had long remained fragmented among diverse, predominantly Muslim merchants, who shared the bounty in relative peace, notwithstanding the danger of pirates. The three principal spices – cloves, nutmeg, and mace – were grown on only a handful of tiny outcroppings in the Molucca and Banda islands north of Australia. Javanese sailors carried them as far as Malacca, on the Malay

Peninsula, to await transshipment, during the monsoon season, to south India. There they joined cargos of pepper, cinnamon, turmeric, cardamom, and dried ginger and galangal heading for the Swahili Coast, the Persian Gulf and the Red Sea. Only a small portion of the harvest passed overland to Cairo and Beirut, whence Italian and Catalan merchants distributed the spices to Europe. But the entry of Portuguese ships into the Indian Ocean began centuries of war to control the lucrative trade.

Asian spices had been prized in Europe since Roman times, but consumption soared in the fourteenth century. Whether inspired by Muslim cuisine, or as a revival of classical practices, spice-filled dishes dominated the tables of nobles and increasingly the middle classes of Italy and the Western Mediterranean. Yet growing demand coincided with tightened supply as Egyptian Mamluks and Ottoman Turks, having supplanted the Byzantine Empire, exacted heavy tolls on trade destined for Christendom.

Responding to market pressures, the Portuguese explored the African coast in search of a seaborne route to the Indies. The mariners developed a lucrative trade in gold dust, malaguetta pepper, ivory, and slaves, even before Bartolomeu Dias rounded the Cape of Good Hope in 1488. But upon reaching India, they found little interest in European merchandise; their only comparative advantage lay in the use of gunpowder. From strategic bases in Goa, Hormuz, and Malacca, Portuguese caravels raided Muslim shipping, capturing the bulk of the spice trade by the 1530s. The newcomers also went directly to the source of production, exploiting rivalries between the sultans of Tidore and Ternate to obtain favorable clove prices. Nevertheless, their naval presence was never sufficient to monopolize the trade entirely, and Muslim merchants skillfully redirected the traffic. A revolt by clove growers in 1570 further undermined Portuguese control.

By the turn of the seventeenth century, declining Portuguese power encouraged privateers from Malaya, Java, Spain, England and Holland to fight for a share of the trade, which had become more lucrative still with the closure of Middle Eastern ports. The Dutch VOC (formed in 1602) ultimately established a rigid monopoly over spice production. In 1621, Governor Jan Pieterszoon Coen acted decisively to forestall native resistance by killing, enslaving, or marooning the entire population of the Banda Islands. The company imported Javanese slaves to grow nutmeg and mace, both products of the same plant. Dutch soldiers and convicts settled in the islands as overseers. The inhabitants of Ternate and Tidore were fortunate by comparison – impoverished but alive – because the Dutch chose to exterminate clove trees in their native environment and replant them in the Lease Islands, west of the Bandas, in order to centralize production. To maintain the monopoly, the company sent expeditions (*hongitochten*) throughout the archipelago to destroy unauthorized spice trees.

The Dutch held off rivals throughout the seventeenth century, even as market conditions gradually worsened. Unlike the principal spices, pepper vines grew widely throughout India and South-east Asia, making a complete monopoly impossible. The VOC therefore manipulated European markets, keeping them slightly oversupplied, to discourage less efficient English and French merchants. The Dutch even came to dominate shipping within Asia, helping the company pay dividends of 20 to 40 percent. Yet the military costs of hegemony proved high, particularly during the mid-century Anglo-Dutch wars. Moreover, the European hunger for spices was finally becoming satiated. Portuguese and Dutch trade empires had made spices accessible to broader segments of European society, thus undermining their social prestige. Although new markets opened in Russia and Poland, consumer tastes had begun a fundamental shift away from heavily spiced foods toward new and sweeter stimulants.

## Sugar and slaves

Sugar held a minor place in the spice chest of medieval Europe, used sparingly to complement other flavors rather than in bulk to impart a distinctively sweet taste. Supplies were relatively plentiful because Muslims had introduced sugar cane to the Mediterranean. After 1492, the plantation complex spread progressively through the Americas, from Hispaniola in the sixteenth century to Brazil in the seventeenth and the British and French Caribbean in the eighteenth. European consumers developed a voracious appetite for sugar, particularly when combined with the stimulating new beverages coffee, tea, and chocolate, which were also grown on tropical plantations. The relentless rise of production severed the personal connections that characterized African slavery, creating instead a system of capitalist agriculture that reduced human life to a disposable economic input.

From modest beginnings in the Canary Islands, colonial plantations developed into highly organized, heavily capitalized, and time-conscious enterprises comparable to nineteenth-century factories. Spanish and Portuguese planters first drafted Native American workers, but massive casualties from disease and overwork led to their replacement by African slaves. Growing and harvesting sugar required not only arduous physical labor but also careful scheduling to maximize production. Cane dried quickly after cutting and had to be sent immediately to the mill, where giant stone rollers, mechanically powered by the eighteenth century, extracted the juice. Skilled slave technicians boiled the syrup down, skimming off impurities, then cast it into cone-shaped blocks. After a few weeks of drying, darker sugars had settled to the bottom, to be used for making rum, while the white crystals at the top were reserved for European markets.

Sugar consumption took hold first among the elite then spread progressively down the social hierarchy. Elaborate sugar sculptures became essential for noble banquets, and already in 1598, Paul Hentzner, a Dutch traveler in England, described black teeth as "a defect the English seem subject to from their too great use of sugar." Although the Dutchman referred to the rich, commoners later began to drink sweetened coffee and tea. Coffee, originally an Ottoman monopoly, became widely available when the Dutch replanted seedlings in Java in 1616. By the eighteenth century, French Haiti had become another major source of production. Chinese tea was likewise substituted by colonial plantations in Ceylon and India.

Economic calculations also governed slave diets as planters purchased rations or allowed slaves access to provisioning grounds depending on sugar-growing conditions. On highly productive islands such as Barbados, rations of corn meal, rice, and salt cod ensured maximum time in the fields. Slaves in Brazil, Martinique, and elsewhere received a free day to cultivate subsistence crops on land unsuited to cane. The nutritional consequences of these systems varied considerably. A single day might be insufficient to raise food, but handouts could also leave slaves hungry. James Stephen described herring rations as "little better than a mass of foetid matter, containing as little nutrition as the brine in which they lie." Disorders that contemporaries described as "dropsy" or the French "*mal d'estomach*" may have been the vitamin deficiency diseases beriberi and pellagra. Malnutrition also contributed to chronic stillbirths, infant mortality, and perhaps the widespread geophagy (dirt eating) among slave women. With such high death rates, plantations imported a total of nearly ten million Africans before abolition in the nineteenth century.

Slaves nevertheless preserved much of their traditional cooking while helping to shape the cuisines of the Americas. The prevalence of pepper pots, black-eyed peas, yams, okra, greens, and palm oil from the southern United States to Brazil testifies to African influences in mansions as well as slave quarters. Carolina rice production employed Asian grains but West African agricultural skills, a point demonstrated by elaborate coastal levies and the reliance on women to mill the seeds with mortar and pestle. Emerging Creole cuisines also incorporated the Native American staple manioc, a tropical root used to make flatbreads and tapioca. To ensure access to familiar foods, slaves defended their rights to provision grounds. In Brazil, the French merchant, L. F. de Tollenare, recalled: "Passing through the forests I sometimes came upon small clearings where the blacks had come secretly to plant a little manioc." After abolition, slave provision grounds became the foundation for an emerging peasantry throughout the region.

## Conclusion

The histories of sugar and spice recall the question, posed earlier by the Columbian Exchange, of why European imperial expansion proved so devastating. Although the Indian Ocean was no idyllic paradise before the Portuguese arrived, Europeans exploited slaves and commerce with far greater brutality than did Afro-Asian societies. Religion and race partially explain these differences. Islamic law encouraged trade by obliging peace between

Muslims, whereas the Portuguese had a crusading spirit. Likewise, Africans never lost sight of the humanity of their servants, in contrast to Europeans, who viewed darker-skinned people as fundamentally different and destined for servitude.

Yet emerging capitalism also shaped European imperialism by reducing African slaves and spice islanders to mere numbers on the balance sheets of businessmen; indeed, VOC Governor Coen was a trained accountant. The transition of sugar from a rare spice to an item of mass consumption placed relentless pressure to increase production, requiring ever greater numbers of slaves. Economic calculations determined the living standards of bondsmen, and the cost of rations to feed them adequately was balanced against the purchase price of new slaves. Moreover, sugar plantations became a model for the production of coffee, tea, and cacao in tropical climates throughout the world, which created still more demand for sucrose. This new and seemingly insatiable hunger ultimately distinguished capitalist production from earlier agrarian systems. Yet however great the appetite for sugar, it formed only one part of the nouvelle cuisines that emerged in the early modern era.

## Further reading

On Africa, James L. Newman, *The Peopling of Africa: A Geographic Interpretation* (New Haven, CT: Yale University Press, 1995); and David Lee Schoenbrun, *A Green Place, A Good Place: Agrarian Change, Gender, and Social Identity in the Great Lakes Region to the 15th Century* (Portsmouth, NH: Heinemann, 1998). For spices, Fernand Braudel, *Civilization and Capitalism: 15th–18th Century*, transl. Siân Reynolds, 3 vols. (New York: Harper & Row, 1979); and Wolfgang Schivelbusch, *Tastes of Paradise: A Social History of Spices, Stimulants, and Intoxicants* trans. David Jacobson (New York: Random House, 1992). On slavery, Sidney W. Mintz, *Sweetness and Power: The Place of Sugar in Modern History* (New York: Penguin, 1985); Kenneth F. Kiple and Virginia Himmelsteib King, *Another Dimension to the Black Diaspora: Diet, Disease, and Racism* (Cambridge: Cambridge University Press, 1981); and Judith A. Carney, *Black Rice: The African Origins of Rice Cultivation in the Americas* (Cambridge, MA: Harvard University Press, 2001).

# Chapter 4

# Nouvelle cuisines

When a modern chef looks at a recipe from medieval Europe, she will quickly notice the changes that have resulted from culinary modernization. Yet the historian seeking to explain the origins of these new cooking styles faces a greater challenge. Perhaps the most basic trend in Europe over the past five centuries has been the movement away from elaborate, heavily spiced dishes toward simpler, more "natural" flavors. Yet Europeans were not the only ones to follow this path, nor did it represent an exclusive route to culinary modernity. This chapter will survey the early modern transformation of diets in France, England, and Japan in order to reveal important connections between everyday eating habits and broader processes of social change.

Cross-cultural comparisons are hampered by the uneven nature of culinary evolution. European nobles of the Middle Ages shared a common cuisine featuring large platters of meat and whole fowl, served roasted or boiled, with elaborately spiced sauces. During the early modern era, middle classes began to challenge aristocratic privilege at the table as elsewhere. Preserving elite status by consuming greater quantities of food – beyond the heroic appetites of medieval lords – was physically impossible, so nobles emphasized refinement instead of bulk, thereby setting a pattern for the future of European cooking. But these refinements differed from one country to the next, creating for the first time uniquely national tastes. Historians must therefore disaggregate multiple trends to determine whether elite cuisines of England and France emerged from cooks following a common path at uneven speeds or whether they arrived at completely separate patterns of "modernity."

The case of Japan shows that quite diverse social arrangements could lead to the common outcome of a cuisine idealizing simple, natural tastes. Although the feudal systems of Western Europe and Japan shared many similar features, economic and political trends began to diverge in the sixteenth century. The samurai retained a monopoly on political power, but their economic fortunes declined, and culinary austerity became an artistic expression of necessity. Meanwhile, disenfranchised Japanese merchants and farmers parlayed their growing wealth into a vibrant and influential popular cuisine.

As this example demonstrates, one should not focus solely on the elite. Coffeehouses also emerged in the early modern period and became vital to the European bourgeoisie. These shops provided an alternative to aristocratic courts and a forum for the middle sectors to demonstrate their own social distinction, apart from both the nobility and the working classes. A parallel tradition emerged in the Japanese teahouse, which developed two separate patterns, an elite tea ceremony, governed by rigid etiquette, and then boisterous shops, frequented by all ranks of society, merchants, workers, and samurai alike. The differing nature of these popular spaces again makes it difficult to generalize about the emergence of social modernity.

## An aristocracy of the fork

French haute cuisine developed in an era of absolutism as monarchs sought to centralize political power at the expense of provincial nobles. Powerful medieval lords had maintained lavish courts and considerable autonomy, but early modern kings gradually asserted the supremacy of Paris, a process culminating with the construction of the opulent palace, Versailles, by Louis XIV (ruled 1643–1715). By enticing aristocrats away from their landed strongholds, the crown transferred power to loyal administrators. Deprived of political duties, nobles sought prestige through cultural pursuits: music, literature, and cooking. Within this courtly environment, gilded medieval banquets gave way to new standards of conspicuous consumption based on discretion and refinement.

Cookbooks offer a valuable source for following culinary fashion, but the chronology of change remains inexact. Some recipes appeared in print only after decades of use in the kitchen, while others represented innovations that did not gain wide acceptance until years later; more than a few proved completely impractical and never reached the dinner table at all. François La Varenne's *The French Chef* (1651) marked a seemingly radical break with earlier cooking styles, but nearly a century had passed since the last original volume was published in France, and he probably summarized techniques that were already common in aristocratic kitchens. The success of La Varenne inspired a flood of cookbooks, each seeking greater novelty. Vincent La Chapelle, for example, entitled his opus, *The Modern Chef* (1733), although it was largely plagiarized from a 1691 work by Massialot, and Menon published a volume of *Nouvelle Cuisine* (1742), thereby popularizing a now-perennial phrase.

This corpus reveals a significant decline in the variety of meats consumed at the same time that vegetables became more plentiful on elite tables. Medieval lords had gorged their way through the animal kingdom, devouring peacocks and storks along with otters and porpoises during Lent. Such exotic creatures were replaced during the early modern period by domesticated livestock, particularly beef, which had formerly been considered indigestible. Vegetables also lost their negative associations, although nobles chose not the cabbages and cereals consumed in bulk by the peasantry but rather artichokes, mushrooms, asparagus, and herbs – plants absent from the typical garden. Social distinctions thus evolved to fit new economic realities; as grazing fields were plowed under to raise wheat, ordinary livestock gained new cachet. Less-nutritious vegetables became a form of conspicuous consumption, demonstrating the aristocracy's freedom from hunger.

Cooking techniques and the organization of menus also changed to reflect new ingredients. Sweet and savory flavors, combined promiscuously in medieval dishes, were separated into distinct courses, with desserts reserved for the end of the meal. Enormous roasts gave way to smaller dishes, often prepared in frying pans, which allowed a new approach to sauce making through the concentration of juices given off during the cooking process. Sauces also became more smooth and subtle, with less vinegar, and thickened with butter and flour (roux) instead of bread crumbs and ground nuts.

The spice trade likewise fell victim to the nouvelle cuisine of the seventeenth century. Humoral beliefs, inherited from Galen, had formerly required spices to balance the hot and cold properties of foods, but new medical theories based on chemistry freed cooks to explore new tastes. Fresh herbs such chives and tarragon gradually replaced cumin, cardamom, and ginger. The primary items of the trade, pepper, clove, and nutmeg, lingered in smaller quantities, while cinnamon was relegated to dessert. Spices simply did not convey aristocratic status when bourgeois families could also afford them.

A transformation of table manners accompanied the refinement of cooking. Guests at a medieval banquet had shared utensils and cups, but individual table settings gradually became the norm. The fork, used in Italy for eating pasta as early as the fourteenth century, spread to France in the seventeenth century, although Louis XIV continued to eat with his fingers. These new forms of courtly behavior, or "courtesy," sought not only to differentiate nobles from coarse peasants but also to limit personal contact, especially the exchange of bodily fluids. A 1674 cookbook, signed L. S. R., summarized the ideals of refined gentility: "Nowadays it is not the prodigious overflowing of dishes, the abundance of ragoûts and gallimaufries, the extraordinary piles of meat which constitute a good table; it is not the confused mixtures of diverse spices, the mountains of roasts," the chef observed. "It is rather the exquisite choice of meats, the finesse with which they are seasoned, the courtesy and neatness with which they are served."

Noble standards of cooking and behavior also began to filter down the social hierarchy. Cookbooks provided one medium for diffusing courtly ideals to middle-class kitchens, and Menon's *The Bourgeois Cook* (1746), directed specifically to a female audience, became the most reprinted text of the eighteenth century. Nouvelle cuisine even reached the urban working classes, who purchased skillets with increasing frequency during the eighteenth century. Thus, Parisian artisans began to substitute quick-fried meats served *au jus* for the slow-cooked stews known as *pot au feu*.

The ascendancy of nouvelle cuisine depended on butchers as well as chefs. Guildsmen honed their skills in carving beef, developing an elaborate hierarchy of cuts during the eighteenth century, with the choicest parts reserved for noble houses. By law, cheaper cuts sold for fixed prices that were within the reach of skilled workers, at least in good times. In this status-conscious society, middling families risked dishonor if given poorer cuts, and shopping for meat entailed a daily struggle between profit-hungry butchers and housekeepers anxious to maintain appearances. Meat cutters also played an essential role in supplying the roast beef of early modern England, but cooking trends differed across the channel.

## English country cooking

While contrasts are commonly made between the foods of England and France – usually to the detriment of the former – such exercises often unfairly compare French haute cuisine with lower-class English cooking. A more balanced appraisal must recognize that the two cuisines developed with considerable overlap and that differing social conditions contributed to distinct cooking styles. The English experience thus provides a useful point of comparison in evaluating French claims to culinary modernity.

Cookbooks and other historical sources point to a number of divergences between these culinary traditions. The consumption of seafood ironically decreased on the island following the Protestant Reformation, and although the English shared the growing continental preference for beef, they tended to serve it roasted or boiled. Moreover, the seventeenth-century invention of pudding cloth – used to steam or boil a cake-like batter of flour, sugar, and dried fruits – made plum and other sweet and savory puddings a standard dish on English tables, in contrast to the French separation of these tastes.

The production of culinary literature indicates further distinctions between France and England. Unlike male chefs on the continent, who gained status and patronage by publishing innovative recipes, English cookbook authors tended to be women, who offered conservative country fare along with practical instructions for preserving foods. These works also showed considerable antipathy toward extravagant courtly cuisine. Hannah Glasse, bestselling author of *The Art of Cookery Made Plain and Easy* (1747), insisted that "if Gentlemen will have French cooks, they must pay for *French* tricks. . . . So much is the blind Folly of this Age, that they would rather be imposed on by a *French* Booby, than give Encouragement to a good English Cook!"

A number of possible explanations have been offered for these national differences. The English insisted that the higher quality of their beef made fancy cooking unnecessary, although many observers – and not just French ones – considered Parisian meat superior to that found in London. Another theory argued that the Reformation stunted English cooking, but the view of food, like sex, as a necessary evil was more common among nineteenth-century

Victorians than seventeenth-century Puritans. In fact, religious denunciations of gluttony applied to drunkenness rather than festival foods. More compelling explanations for culinary differences emerge from political and social conditions, particularly the Civil War (1642–1649) and "Glorious Revolution" (1688), which thwarted the rise of English absolutism. Nobles retained genuine power in Parliament and thus took less interest in the affectations of courtly life.

Nevertheless, differences between the two cuisines may well be overstated. Nationalist statements notwithstanding, continental chefs had considerable influence across the Channel. Native English cooking traditions may also have been evolving naturally in directions similar to those of the French, with greater use of vegetables, more pan-cooked meats, and sauces based on butter. Even as elite cuisines evolved on largely parallel paths, the middle classes of both England and France began to express themselves through the distinctive culture of the coffeehouse.

## Coffee and the public sphere

European travelers first encountered coffee in the Ottoman Empire during the fifteenth century, but the beverage did not spread west for nearly two hundred years. The Muslim stimulant suddenly became fashionable in Europe as the rising middle classes sought new centers of sociability outside exclusive aristocratic courts. Coffeehouses became the hub of an emerging public sphere, where people freely voiced opinions on business, the arts, and politics. These new intellectual discussions in turn challenged absolutist monarchs and became a vital forum for democratic government.

Introduced to England about 1650, at the height of Puritan influence, coffee quickly replaced beer among businessmen, who gathered each morning over steaming cups to read newspapers and conduct deals. Edward Lloyd's London coffeehouse, for example, attracted merchants and ship captains, whose exchange of maritime information led to the founding of a prominent insurance brokerage. Journalists had their own favorite shops, and newspapers were written as well as read over cups of java. Coffeehouses in market towns subscribed to London papers, thus spreading news and political discussions throughout the country. In the eighteenth century, tea gradually eclipsed coffee as the national drink, encouraged by the vigorous advertising campaigns of the British East India Company; nevertheless, coffeehouses provided the setting for an emerging parliamentary political culture.

The first coffeehouses opened in Paris at about the same time as those in London, but they gained popularity only in the mid-eighteenth century, as the public began to challenge absolute monarchy. In 1782, Le Grand d'Aussy observed:

> There is not a single bourgeois home in which coffee is not served, not a single shopkeeper, cook, or chambermaid who does not take *café au lait* in

the morning. In public markets on some of the capital's streets and byways there are women who sell the rabble what they call *café au lait*, which is really bad milk stained with used coffee grinds.

Coffeehouses offered meeting places for the Enlightenment *philosophes* Voltaire, Diderot, and less famous names of the French literary underground. During the historic days of 1789, Camille Desmoulins and his fellow revolutionary leaders gathered over coffee in the arcades of the Palais Royal to plan the assault on the Bastille and the overthrow of the dictatorship.

In explaining the associations between coffeehouses, capitalism, and parliamentary democracy, one cannot ignore the physiological effects of caffeine in stimulating mental activity. Some have gone further, linking coffee with a Protestant work ethic, but this argument fails to explain its popularity in Catholic France. Class, rather than religion, provides a more likely point of connection; the bourgeoisie took up coffee in order to appear sober and hardworking, thus justifying their claims to political power in place of either idle aristocrats or drunken laborers. Yet there was nothing automatic about these class associations, as can be seen in Japanese society.

## "The way of the cutting knife"

With its emphasis on skilled carving, the Japanese art of cooking may sound like a gastronomic sideline for the samurai elite, similar to the genteel pursuits of the French aristocracy, but social trends of the Tokugawa Shogunate (1603–1868) defy easy comparison with early modern Europe. The dynasty restored order after a century of civil wars, transforming samurai warriors into a bureaucratic class. The advent of peace allowed economic prosperity, particularly for urban merchants, ostensibly at the bottom of the social hierarchy. Over time, the samurai living on fixed stipends lost purchasing power as a result of inflation. The growing confusion between status, wealth, and power helped to produce a thriving popular cuisine, enjoyed by nobles and commoners alike, even as the samurai cultivated an austere culinary aesthetic.

Japanese food developed its modern form beginning in the twelfth century, when individual place settings were first arranged on low wooden trays. A meal comprised bowls of rice, soup, and small side dishes of fish and vegetables. As court cuisine grew more elaborate, cooking schools (*ryū*) emerged among Japanese master chefs, who guarded their secrets jealously, handing them down only to trusted disciples. Ceremonial robes and tall, black-lacquered hats heightened their prestige, and cutting knives were made with the same folded-steel used for samurai swords. Each school cultivated distinctive carving styles, often of maddening complexity; for example, the Shijō-ryū supposedly perfected thirty-six ways of cutting carp.

During the Tokugawa era, these cooking schools were formalized and simplified according to the minimalist principles of Japanese gardening. Chefs composed slices of fish in asymmetrical arrangements with strips of daikon radish piled to resemble a mountain or greens arrayed like a small forest. The sixteenth-century introduction of soy sauce contributed to food artistry by allowing affluent diners to dip each bite individually. To complement their elegant presentations, chefs avoided piquant, spicy foods. This quest for natural flavors led to the adoption of a Zen Buddhist maxim: "Not to cook is the ideal of cooking."

The popular classes meanwhile developed their own lively dining traditions within the cities, particularly the capital, Edo. Male migrant workers from the countryside created a demand for inexpensive prepared food, and the first soba (buckwheat) noodle shops opened in the mid-seventeenth century. Tempura and grilled eel with sweet sauce were also sold in shops, stalls, and by ambulant vendors in the streets. Around 1800, cooks wearing hand towels . wrapped around their heads and outlandish striped kimonos and jackets began combining rice balls with bits of fresh fish; this new fad for sushi quickly spread from Edo to other cities.

Social distinctions between elites and commoners, in theory quite rigid but often blurred in practice, were also apparent in teahouses. First opened around temples and shrines in the fifteenth century, they spread along roadsides everywhere, serving light meals and restorative teas. In eighteenth-century Edo, teahouses also flourished around theaters and sumo arenas, often selling more *sake* than tea, while other locations evolved into high-class restaurants. The favorite teahouses were in the "floating world" of the Yoshiwara pleasure district, on the banks of the Sumida River, where fresh seafood was readily available and geisha performed songs and dances. Although rigid rules of etiquette governed the formal tea ceremony, prominent samurai often preferred the more boisterous atmosphere of the brothels.

In Tokugawa Japan, culinary innovation moved both up and down the social hierarchy. Elite foods spread out from the court as individual banquet settings were adopted by commoners. By the eighteenth century, secrets of exclusive *ryū* had leaked out through publication in cookbooks, which had to compete with popular texts such as *A Hundred Tofu Curiosities* (1782). Moreover, the cash-strapped samurai elite indulged in the popular cuisine of soba and sushi. All ranks of society, from laborers to businessmen and politicians, mingled freely in the pleasure quarters. Far from a closed feudal society, early modern Japan possessed a degree of cultural fluidity that facilitated its later industrialization.

## Conclusion

The common culinary ideal of simple, natural food appeared in France, England, and Japan during periods of wide-ranging modernization, but each country attached different social and aesthetic significance to these changes. An exclusive French aristocracy pursued culinary simplification, which they associated with the naturalism of neo-classical art. The English meanwhile largely rejected the fussiness they perceived in French court cuisine and sought a simpler, country cooking appropriate to their more fluid social hierarchy. In practice, many similarities emerged between the two, although the evidence suggests two rival interpretations. English cookbook authors may have mimicked French practices even while protesting their nationalist credentials, or else the two cuisines simply followed parallel trajectories. After all, culinary simplification occurred in Japan under quite different conditions, in which elite and popular traditions overlapped, even as the samurai cultivated social distinction through an austere Zen aesthetic.

Theorizing connections between nouvelle cuisines and social modernization becomes even more difficult as the examples multiply. The few available cooking manuscripts from the eighteenth-century Middle East indicate that foods may have been undergoing a comparable process of simplification, but at a time of extremely limited social change. Mexico, although influenced by the political and economic transformations of the Enlightenment, did not abandon the spicy, complex chile pepper stews of the colonial period in favor of simpler dishes fashionable in Europe. Thus, the associations discussed in this chapter must necessarily remain speculative until more data become available from around the world. Future research must also address the popular masses as well as elite dining habits, for the eighteenth century was a time of changing economic patterns, in which traditional provisioning networks gave way to new market systems.

## Further reading

On European cookery, Jean-Louis Flandrin, "Dietary Choices and Culinary Technique, 1500–1800," in Jean-Louis Flandrin and Massimo Montanari (eds), *Food: A Culinary History from Antiquity to the Present*, trans. Albert Sonnenfeld (New York: Columbia University Press, 1999); Stephen Mennell, *All Manners of Food: Eating and Taste in England and France from the Middle Ages to the Present* (Oxford: Basil Blackwell, 1985); and Sydney Watts, *Meat Matters: The Butchers of Old Regime Paris* (Rochester, NY: University of Rochester Press, forthcoming). For coffee culture, Wolfgang Schivelbusch, *Tastes of Paradise: A Social History of Spices, Stimulants, and Intoxicants*, trans. David Jacobson (New York: Random House, 1992). On Japan, Nishiyama Matsunosuke, *Edo Culture: Daily Life and Diversions in Urban Japan, 1600–1868*, trans. Gerald Groemer (Honolulu: University of Hawai'i Press, 1997); and Susan B. Hanley, *Everyday Things in Premodern Japan: The Hidden Legacy of Material Culture* (Berkeley, CA: University of California Press, 1997).

# Chapter 5

# Moral and political economies

Food riots had long been a common form of popular protest, but they reached new intensity worldwide in the eighteenth century, precisely when food supplies were becoming more dependable overall. In 1789, Parisian women marched on Versailles to drag "the Baker" – Louis XVI – back to the capital and thus guarantee access to bread. Muslim women had staged an equally symbolic protest four decades earlier by occupying the minaret of Aleppo's Great Mosque during prayer to hurl abuse at the Ottoman governor for negligence in times of famine. When the town council of Querétaro, Mexico, could not stem the high price of food in 1749, a mob rampaged through the streets and attacked the public granary. China maintained the most comprehensive granary system of the pre-modern world, but nevertheless, crowds of hungry people regularly looted storehouses and blocked shipments of rice. To understand this seeming paradox of protest in a time of rising expectations, it is necessary to examine the politics of provisioning from a global perspective.

Devastating famines, which had plagued Western Europe as late as the seventeenth century, were largely overcome by eighteenth-century improvements in agriculture and marketing. People began to expect more from life than dreary subsistence as greater food production lowered infant mortality and relieved chronic hunger. Conditions varied regionally, but the culmination of the Columbian Exchange fueled population growth around the world. Between 1650 and 1850, China's population tripled from roughly 140,000,000 to more than 425,000,000, aided by the diffusion of American sweet potatoes, maize, and peanuts. These crops also spread through Africa, although without the same demographic effects because of the continued drain of the Atlantic slave trade, which reached its peak in the eighteenth century. Meanwhile, Latin America's population finally began to recover from the conquest, causing the diversion of land from livestock to grain.

Nevertheless, the distribution of food was just as important as its production. If the poor had no legal entitlement to available grain, then hunger and social unrest were sure to follow. In medieval Europe, the Catholic Church demanded a "moral economy" and condemned merchants who overcharged consumers for basic foods. During normal times, the "just" price was simply the market price, but when famine struck, authorities were morally bound to intervene in the market and guarantee subsistence for the poor. Such paternalistic action was essential for ensuring stability in rigidly hierarchical societies, not only in Europe but around the world. Conquistadors carried the notion of a just price to the Americas, where reciprocity was already well established. Confucian teachings demanded a similar concern for the poor, as did Islamic requirements of charity.

These traditional relationships came under increasing pressure from social changes of the eighteenth century. The extension of the commercial economy into the European countryside unsettled the old order by diverting subsistence agriculture to market crops, uprooting peasants to create a mobile but marginal workforce, and encouraging grain sales directly from landed gentry to urban merchants. Food riots broke out when local notables shipped scarce grain to the cities instead of feeding it to local dependants, thus responding to the capitalist logic of a new "political economy" instead of the paternalistic responsibilities of the established moral economy. Abandoned by their leaders, the crowds therefore acted autonomously to enforce the traditional practices. Markets played an equally important role in distributing food in both the Chinese and Ottoman Empires, yet these governments remained far more concerned with preserving social stability. The resulting food riots, although superficially similar to those in Europe, reflected tensions within established hierarchies rather than conservative reactions to new conditions. Even in Europe, governments differed in their responses to capitalist transformation, creating alternative versions of political economy. The British ruling class developed a profound faith in unfettered markets to allocate resources efficiently, whereas the French elite insisted on the role of the state in guiding the development of free trade while still ensuring adequate subsistence for all.

## The hunger of early capitalism

Grain seizures occurred in many locations in eighteenth-century Europe, on farms, highways, and canals, but perhaps most commonly, food riots broke out in markets and bakeries. Women gathered to purchase their family's daily bread only to discover that prices had risen beyond their means to pay. Harsh words were exchanged, and if the merchant refused to offer a discount, the crowd proceeded to ransack the shop while nevertheless paying what they considered a reasonable sum, a practice called *taxation populaire* in France. Magistrates intervened, but usually lacked sufficient force to quell the uprisings; the best they could achieve was an orderly distribution of grain with a minimum of property damage. Complaints by merchants and officials notwithstanding, these riots were not spasmodic, instinctive outbursts by hungry mobs. Instead, the crowds generally acted in a rational manner, according to time-honored practices, and with the goal of persuading local elites to fulfill their paternalistic responsibilities.

Agricultural improvements provided the setting for eighteenth-century food riots. The enclosure movement turned communal fields into private property, allowing wealthy farmers to accumulate large productive tracts while many peasants were reduced to wage labor. Rapidly growing cities devoured correspondingly greater supplies of grain, but even villages became more dependent on markets instead of subsistence cultivation. Meanwhile, large landowners increasingly sold grain directly to urban merchants. By the 1770s, liberal regimes facilitated this long-distance trade by abolishing medieval laws against forestalling, the practice of withholding grain from local markets in the hopes of selling it for higher prices.

The prospect of grain being carried away from hungry villages provoked outrage and violence. The 1774 liberalization of the French grain trade by the Controller General Turgot coincided with a poor harvest, launching a widespread insurrection known as the Flour War. Women often took the lead in inciting these urban food riots; Marie Louise Jardin punched a grain merchant in Beaumont-sur-Oise while pregnant and ready to give birth. She got off with only a reprimand, like many women, whose actions were condoned by officials as fulfilling their domestic duties. By contrast, men made up the crowds who invaded wealthy farms and seized grain in transit by cart or ferry – the fields and highways being considered male spaces. If arrested, they faced harsh prison sentences or even the gallows. These crowds nevertheless believed their cause to be just and acted with a notable sense of common purpose.

Undisturbed by a century of grain riots, the British elite acquired a growing faith in the political economy of free markets to guarantee public welfare. In *The Wealth of Nations* (1776), Adam Smith dismissed the prejudice against forestalling as a superstition that impeded a properly functioning economy. Thomas Malthus wrote *An Essay on the Principle of Population* (1798) to show that human reproduction always outran agricultural productivity over the long run. Only natural catastrophes – famine, disease, and warfare – could control population growth. Believing that higher wages simply encouraged the working classes to have more babies, many nineteenth-century liberals concluded grimly that efforts to alleviate poverty were ultimately futile.

French rulers shared the Smithian belief in markets as an efficient means of distributing grain, but without the same confidence in their ability to function unaided by the state. Throughout the eighteenth century, local officials engaged in surreptitious grain sales to hold down prices but without deterring merchants from their work. During the revolutionary upheavals after 1789, policy swung wildly between radical liberalization and draconian price controls. The failures of both extremes demonstrated the need for more sophisticated state action to create market incentives while still satisfying the immediate needs of hungry consumers. The restored monarchy developed an elaborate system of grain reserves and credit mechanisms to avoid market failures in times of crisis, and the relaxation of these regulations may have contributed to the turmoil of 1848. By the 1860s, free trade in grain had been achieved, not by the market but by state intervention. Thus, France pursued a more active political economy of food distribution than did England, yet even the French elite seemed indifferent compared to the Chinese zeal for public service.

## China's ever-normal granary

Although founded by Manchu invaders, the Qing dynasty (1644–1911) sought to preserve intact the customs of their Chinese subjects. The Kangxi emperor (ruled 1661–1722) conquered vast stretches of Mongolia, Central Asia, and Tibet, but he was also a dedicated Confucian scholar responsible for establishing a civilian granary system ultimately comprising a million tons of grain. Fearing social disruption from the unbridled pursuit of wealth, officials did not hesitate to intervene in grain markets to ensure famine relief. Chinese governors nevertheless recognized the vital role of merchants in distributing grain. With an enormous population hovering on the brink of subsistence, officials could not completely balance competing claims for food, leading to outbreaks of violence.

The ever-normal granaries reached their peak of operation in the mid-eighteenth century and alleviated distress among peasants who had formerly relied on usurious loans from merchants to survive the lean spring months. Local magistrates offered low-interest loans of grain to poor families and were repaid at harvest, which provided a regular turnover so that grain did not rot in storage. The provincial bureaucracy also mobilized reserves in case of natural disasters by shipping grain to famine-stricken regions. Yet Qing emperors never envisioned the ever-normal granary system as a replacement for private commerce. The system had limited impact in regions already well served by markets, such as the Yangzi valley or the capital, Beijing. Merchants also retained a vital intermediary role transporting food from areas of surplus to those where prices were high; bureaucrats only began redistributing reserves when market failures threatened widespread starvation.

As in Europe, the prospect of grain being carried off to distant markets provoked food riots by hungry crowds. During a shortage of 1742 and 1743, Chen Hongmou, governor of Jiangxi Province, attributed popular grain seizures to the greed of rich landowners and merchants: "They believe rice prices will continue to rise. Hence they are unwilling to sell at current prices." Yet officials could not completely block the transportation of grain without risking even greater distress. Food riots in eighteenth-century China arose out of the uneasy coexistence of local and long-distance markets, unlike contemporary European uprisings, incited by the transition between subsistence and capitalist markets.

By the end of the eighteenth century, moreover, the granary system had begun to decline, along with the Qing dynasty. Increasing military demands to suppress rebellions competed with civilian needs, and graft and incompetence proliferated among local magistrates. The resulting unrest paralleled the situation of another declining empire at the other end of the Asian continent.

## The Ottoman Empire

At their height in the sixteenth century, Ottoman sultans held sway from the Balkans to the Persia Gulf and across North Africa. These powerful rulers had carefully overseen urban provisioning; indeed, their status within the Muslim world depended in large part on guaranteeing regular food supplies to the holy cities of Mecca and Medina. In the eighteenth century, the central government began losing control of tax revenues to local potentates. Public services within the empire had always depended on private charity, but the weakened state became increasingly unable to assure supplies of food from the countryside. Ordinary people, bedeviled by corrupt governors, protested vainly for relief in times of scarcity.

The sultans' inability to police the empire contributed to declining agriculture and population at a time of unprecedented growth elsewhere in the world. During good years, the productive fields of Anatolia, Egypt, and Syria could support the cities, but the government restricted grain transfers between provinces, so local harvest failures caused considerable suffering. Meanwhile, peasants labored under indebtedness and fear of Bedouin and Kurdish nomads. Farmers often turned to brigandage or fled to the cities, and by the end of the eighteenth century, even wealthy agricultural provinces regularly failed to supply the needs of the local population.

For city dwellers, official graft compounded the problems of rural unrest and bad harvests. Governments decreed price controls but did little to enforce them, and local magistrates often profited personally from the grain trade. During the famine of 1787, Janissary officers in Aleppo set themselves up as middlemen, reselling food on the black market. When crowds of protesters assembled outside the *shari'a* courts, troops dispersed them. Without support from the local elite, the poor had little chance of making their voices heard. The Ottoman case shows that a stable government was necessary to ensure the well-being of the people, but it was not a sufficient condition, as became apparent in Ireland.

## The Irish potato famine

Rain and frost had ravaged potato crops before, but no one in 1845 foresaw the extent of the tragedy when an American fungus, *Phytophthora infestans*, struck the dietary staple of three million Irish farmers. They eked their way through the winter, then planted the tubers that survived, only to see the blight return with the first rains. The 1846 potato crop was a complete loss, and in December newspapers reported: "Disease and death in every quarter – the once hardy population worn away to emaciated skeletons – fever, dropsy, diarrhoea,

and famine rioting in every filthy hovel, and sweeping away whole families."
By 1850, nearly 100,000 people had died of nutritional disease or outright
starvation, while another 500,000 succumbed to infection. Total mortality
during the famine years surpassed 1 million, and an equal number migrated
from Ireland. Yet the greatest irony of all was the success of local grain harvests,
for even as people died in the streets, ships embarked from Irish ports with
food bound for English markets.

In the sixteenth century, Ireland was a pastoral country with about a million
inhabitants subsisting largely on dairy products. When English invaders
took over the land, the Irish fed themselves on newly introduced potatoes. The
Andean tuber proved well suited to the soil, and between 1700 and 1845, the
population quadrupled from about 2 million to 8.5 million. By the nineteenth century, the Irish masses had become completely dependent on
this single source of food. Working men regularly consumed ten pounds a day,
washed down with milk. Yet this healthy if monotonous diet proved tragically
vulnerable to sudden infestation.

For many observers, the Great Famine confirmed the grim conclusions
of Malthus. Cheap potatoes had encouraged population growth far beyond
the long-term carrying capacity of the soil. Famines had struck already
in 1740, 1799, and 1816, and crop failures became more frequent in the
1820s and 1830s. According to this interpretation, Ireland was destined to
starve. Nevertheless, the island was not densely populated by continental
standards, and even Malthus had not foreseen the disaster: "Although it is
quite certain that the population of Ireland cannot continue permanently to
increase at its present rate, yet it is as certain that it will not *suddenly* come
to a stop."

However great the failure of nature, it was matched by a failure of politics.
Parliament had enacted a Poor Law in 1838, but Ireland's starving masses
completely overwhelmed the system. Prison diets were actually superior to
those of the workhouses, and inmates of the latter often turned to crime to get
more food; prison officials eventually lowered rations to reduce the temptation
to steal. In 1847, the government opened a number of soup kitchens, then
closed them within six months, prolonging the tragedy through the end of
the decade. Nor would the prime minister consider a ban on grain exports from
the island. The destruction of the potato crop was so sudden and complete that
nothing could have averted the crisis entirely, but English devotion to *laissez-
faire* political economy compounded the suffering of millions of Irish people.

## Conclusion

Eighteenth-century experience clearly demonstrates that starvation was as
much a problem of distribution as of production. Harvest failure triggered the
outbreak of crisis, but its consequences were determined by pre-existing
political and economic arrangements. Hunger inspired the outrage of crowds,

but popular expectations likewise shaped the course of the food riots that followed.

Popular well-being depended equally on the effectiveness of markets and on the responsibility of the government. The Ottoman Empire, in its decline, illustrated the vicious circle that could take hold of provisioning, when officials came to profit from the distress of their subjects. By contrast, the Chinese case showed that a government committed to social welfare could feed its population even as their numbers strained the ecological limits of the land. Effective markets were critical to the efficient distribution of grain, but they alone could not guarantee the welfare of the poorest segments of a society, as the Irish potato famine proved so tragically.

The crucial role of provisioning can also help to rethink accepted notions about Europe's place in world history. Scholars often contrast European dynamism with Chinese decadence in the early modern era. If both regions suffered comparable food riots but only the West made the transition to modernity as a result, one might conclude that social disruption was a price worth paying. Yet one should not exaggerate the differences between a "traditional" moral economy and a "modern" political economy, for both sought to balance political morality and merchant economics. Moreover, this argument fails to account for demographic differences. China could not have followed a *laissez-faire* approach without allowing untold millions to starve. By the same token, had English parliamentarians studied the Confucian classics, might the worst of the potato famine have been avoided?

Whether governed wisely or poorly, pre-modern societies existed under the constraints made possible by agricultural productivity. Until the rise of industry, economic growth remained primarily a function of population. The transition to a modern world promised most of all relief from hunger, yet the specter of Malthus continued to haunt even affluent industrial societies.

## Further reading

On Europe, E. P. Thompson, "The Moral Economy of the English Crowd in the Eighteenth Century," *Past and Present* 50 (1971): 76–136; Steven Laurence Kaplan, *Provisioning Paris: Merchants and Millers in the Grain and Flour Trade during the Eighteenth Century* (Ithaca, NY: Cornell University Press, 1984); Cynthia A. Bouton, *The Flour War: Gender, Class, and Community in Late Ancien Régime French Society* (University Park, PA: Pennsylvania State University Press, 1993); Judith A. Miller, *Mastering the Market: The State and the Grain Trade in Northern France, 1700–1860* (Cambridge: Cambridge University Press, 1999); and L. A. Clarkson and E. Margaret Crawford, *Feast and Famine: Food and Nutrition in Ireland 1500–1920* (Oxford: Oxford University Press, 2001). For Chinese comparisons, Pierre-Étienne Will and R. Bin Wong, *Nourish the People: The State Civilian Granary System in China, 1650–1850* (Ann Arbor, MI: University of Michigan Center for Chinese Studies, 1991); and R. Bin Wong, *China Transformed: Historical Change and the Limits of European Experience* (Ithaca, NY: Cornell University Press, 1997). On the Ottoman

Empire, Rhoads Murphey, "Provisioning Istanbul: The State and Subsistence in the Early Modern Middle East," *Food and Foodways* 2 (1988): 217–63; and Abraham Marcus, *The Middle East on the Eve of Modernity: Aleppo in the Eighteenth Century* (New York: Columbia University Press, 1989).

# Part II

# The taste of modernity

The early modern diffusion of foodstuffs increased agricultural productivity and population growth throughout the world, but most people still cooked and ate in basically the same ways that they had before. Nineteenth-century industrialization, by contrast, radically transformed the preparation – even the fundamental nature – of food. Railroads and steamships brought fruits, vegetables, and meat to market from across continents and oceans, altering supply networks not only in Western Europe and North America but also in the most remote areas of Africa, Asia, Australia, and Latin America. Meanwhile, industrial technology increasingly removed cooking from home kitchens to distant factories. These changes had wide-ranging social repercussions.

By harnessing inanimate energy sources and reorganizing production methods, industrialization accelerated the pace of modern life. The factory system first transformed the workplace, replacing the self-made pace of agricultural labor with the relentless rhythms of the machine. The slaughterhouse offers a particularly dramatic example of this new mode of production. No longer did skilled craftsmen carve meat from freshly butchered animals for waiting consumers. Instead, teams of proletarian workers performed repetitive tasks, mechanically carving up livestock in Midwestern factories for shipment, either in cans or refrigerated railroad cars, to distant markets. Over the following century, countless other industries, ranging from bread to beer and from canned fruits to frozen vegetables, achieved similar efficiencies. Mass production thus greatly increased the quantities of food and other consumer goods available to workers. Indeed, they became necessary with the rapid growth of urbanization, which left traditional sources of supply inadequate to meet modern demands.

Yet this new consumer culture brought anxiety alongside abundance. The commoditization of foods created abstract forms of economic exchange – futures markets for winter wheat that was still unplanted or for hog bellies that had not yet been slaughtered – leaving farmers at the mercy of new profiteers and speculators. Because consumers no longer had direct access to the source of their foods, they had to find new methods of determining the wholesomeness of what they ate. Commercial brand names substituted for local merchants, thus transforming the pre-modern moral economy and placing new demands on government oversight. Gender roles were likewise unsettled as women abandoned domestic production and entered the industrial workforce.

Meanwhile, political modernity took shape in a series of revolutions that toppled monarchs and replaced them with nation states. Insurgents throughout the Atlantic world began to repudiate elite privilege and demand more democratic forms of government. Court culture likewise fell victim to the ideal of popular sovereignty, as the newly empowered middle classes began to assert the validity of their own tastes in contrast to the hereditary nobility. The French Revolution of 1789 created the first national cuisine, as restaurants, cookbooks, and other gastronomic literature made elite dining increasingly available to the popular sectors. Yet the French left a complex legacy, on the one hand, encouraging other nations to harness food to the goal of national unity, while, on the other, providing a new and exclusive dining culture that allowed other national elites to differentiate themselves from the local masses. Such social contradictions frustrated many attempts to forge national cuisines in the nineteenth century. In the United States, by contrast, the national cuisine became conflated not with elite cooking but rather with the mass market of industrial cuisine.

National rivalries also combined with industrial production to encourage European powers to assert hegemony over most of the world. Advances in military technology, medical knowledge, and communications and transportation allowed relatively small imperial armies to defeat superior numbers of African and Asian opponents. Meanwhile in North and South America, settlers used these same advantages to expel indigenous peoples from fertile lands. As a result of imperial expansion, the western powers gained control of vast stretches of territory for tropical plantations and livestock raising, thereby providing the material basis for Western dietary abundance.

Europeans also used the newly developed science of nutrition to justify their expanding global reach. The faith in their own cultural superiority, which had previously inspired Spanish conquistadors and missionaries to implant wheat and livestock in the Americas, helped convince the nineteenth-century imperial powers, Britain and France, of the benevolent nature of colonial rule. Nutritional rationales were also employed at home to justify the exclusion of migrant workers, who were unaccustomed to the carnivorous diet of Western Europe. These supposedly scientific arguments were based not on solid medical evidence but rather on the racial and cultural preconceptions of the dominant classes. Moreover, colonial rulers did little in practice to improve the nutritional health of their subjects.

Nevertheless, the globalization of food in the nineteenth century was not solely the product of imperial power. Indeed, colonial rulers often acquired a taste for the foods of their subjects. Indian curry and chutney, for example, became mainstays of the British diet. The proletarian migrations that provided labor for industrialization also contributed to the diffusion of food habits in this period. While French chefs acquired international fame, more humble Chinese and Italian cooks performed the bulk of the labor, even in ostensibly French kitchens.

# Chapter 6

# The industrial kitchen

Before the nineteenth century, only the elite could enjoy white bread and meat on a daily basis. With the rise of industrial mass production, these and many other foods have come to be regarded as everyday staples in Western society. Yet while fears of starvation have passed, the modern diet has created a host of new uncertainties.

Scholars have long debated whether industrialization allowed ordinary workers to live and eat better. There is general consensus that most people in Britain saw few benefits from the changes between 1750 and 1820, while incomes generally rose in the period after 1850. Controversy still surrounds the intermediate years; some factory workers earned considerably higher wages, but with inflation and rising inequality, two-thirds of the British population may have struggled to survive on stagnant incomes. Indeed, the consumption of staple grains, meat, tea, and sugar increased little before the mid-1840s. Workers in continental Europe and the United States faced similar deprivations, as entire generations missed out on the "trickle-down" of industrial wealth.

When nutrition did improve for common people, it came at the price of a growing distance between producer and consumer. Urban dwellers had always depended on food supplies from a more or less distant countryside and had to beware of profiteering merchants and unscrupulous adulteration. Nevertheless, the meaning of "wholesome" changed fundamentally as foods began arriving by railroad and steamship from around the world. The freshness of meat was no longer determined by how recently it had been slaughtered but rather by its packaging and refrigeration. Shoppers, who formerly judged the quality of foods for themselves by smell and touch, increasingly had to trust the label on a can. Farmers, meanwhile, began selling to giant warehouses at a standard rate instead of shipping to market individual sacks that were priced according to the plumpness and purity of the grain. Foods became interchangeable commodities, losing all connection to their place of origin.

Industrialization further shifted the global balance of power, a process begun with the Columbian Exchange, by allowing Europeans to exploit more efficiently the material wealth of distant continents. The vast temperate plains of

Australia, Argentina, Canada, and the United States were transformed into bread baskets and grazing lands to feed the growing ranks of factory workers. Tropical regions likewise contributed ever greater quantities of sugar, chocolate, coffee, and tea, as well as bananas and other fruits previously unavailable in northern climes. Although Europeans reaped the greatest benefits from new technologies, non-Western people were not completely dependent on the industrial powers. Students traveled from Africa, Asia, and the Americas to learn new scientific methods, which they then applied to the foods of their homelands. Thus, nineteenth-century Mexican inventors mechanized corn milling even as Nigerian farmers modernized the production of palm oil.

## New technologies

The factory system, designed to achieve mass production through mechanization, found ready application in the food processing industry. New methods of preservation, particularly canning and refrigeration, allowed such economies of scale that factories could produce enough to feed whole cities without spoilage or waste. Steam engines powered giant mills as well as ships and trains that carried industrial products across continents and oceans. In sheer quantities, the foods available to late nineteenth-century British and North American cities outstripped all previous supply systems in history.

Since ancient times, the Chinese had used salt on a large scale to preserve fish and soy sauce, and North Atlantic salt cod improved European diets in the sixteenth century, but the invention of canning by Nicolas Appert around 1809 brought food into the industrial age. The Parisian confectioner discovered how to prevent decay by boiling foods in sealed glass bottles. The British quickly adapted the technique to sturdier tin cans, which soon became standard rations on board British Navy ships. Consumer demand grew more slowly, because of both high initial costs and the lack of an efficient can opener – hammer and chisel were needed at first. Nevertheless, by the 1830s, European and U.S. shops began stocking canned fish and meat, followed later by fruits and vegetables.

Mass production also depended on an efficient division of labor, particularly for the first meatpackers in the Midwestern United States. Founded in Cincinnati about 1830, this industry employed teams of specialized workers, each of whom performed a single, repetitive task, cutting away a ham or a side of bacon, until the hog vanished completely at the end of this "disassembly line." Frederick Law Olmsted observed: "No iron cog-wheels could work with more regular motion. Plump falls the hog upon the table, chop, chop; chop, chop; chop, chop, fall the cleavers. All is over." Once packed in barrels of brine, the meat was shipped east by barge. At first, the industry was limited to the winter months, when freezing temperatures slowed the process of decay, but by the 1850s the arrival of railroads and ice harvesting had extended production year round. During the Civil War, access to hogs fattened on corn from Iowa and Nebraska allowed Chicago to replace Cincinnati as the meatpacking capital, "Porkopolis."

The marketing of grain likewise benefited from new forms of standardization made possible by the grain elevator, an enormous vertical warehouse, invented in 1842, with steam-powered conveyor belts that poured cereal in from the top and chutes below that dropped it into waiting ships or railroad cars. Gravity moved grain more efficiently than any stevedore could manage with burlap sacks, and Chicago's massive elevators dominated world markets by the late 1850s. Without the sacks, grains from individual farms were mixed indiscriminately, and the arbitrary dividing line between, say, first and second-class spring wheat often meant the difference between survival and bankruptcy for Midwestern farmers. Railroads stimulated production in other temperate regions as well; in the 1880s the vast pampas grasslands of Argentina were converted to agriculture, although farmers remained at the mercy of grain merchants such as Ernesto "the Octopus" Bunge. The global fall in wheat prices, which ruined countless growers, nevertheless provided cheap bread for factory workers.

At the same time, improved milling technology meant more refined foods. Traditional millstones had simply pulverized wheat, leaving behind bits of hull and oils that quickly went rancid. Hungarian roller-mills, pioneered in the 1840s, progressively removed the outer layers of the grain, yielding purer, whiter flour. Meanwhile, British engineers updated rice milling machinery, which encouraged the importation of unprocessed paddy rice instead of previously milled grain from Asia – an example of European industrialization causing de-industrialization elsewhere. Even chocolate milling was improved in 1828 with the Dutch invention of a press to remove excess cocoa butter, creating a smoother drinking chocolate and contributing later to mass-produced confectionery. Ordinary people could now buy former luxury foods, although white bread and rice were actually less nutritious than darker, whole-grain versions.

Mechanical refrigeration offered another critical breakthrough, allowing urban consumers greater access to fresh beef. Unlike pork, which took well to curing, beef became hard and tasteless when salted and dried. As a result, cattle in Argentina, Australia, and Texas were often slaughtered for their hides, with the meat left to rot. In 1867, cowboys opened the Chisholm Trail, driving Texas longhorns north to the railhead at Abilene, Kansas, for shipment to eastern markets. Yet live cattle transport had barely begun when George Hammond first shipped beef by railroad icebox; within a decade, refrigerated rail cars had become economical. Applying the same industrial techniques used for hogs, the Chicago meatpacking firms of Hammond, Swift, and Armour soon dominated the U.S. beef trade, underselling local butchers who tried to compete with freshly slaughtered beef. The packers also gained a major share of the British market because Australian and Argentine meat had to be frozen solid, and therefore fetched lower prices than North American chilled beef.

Industrial foods achieved widespread consumer acceptance through a commercial revolution of advertising and retailing. In the 1870s, Glasgow merchant, Thomas Lipton built a grocery store empire selling affordable canned goods, while the Atlantic and Pacific Tea Company opened "economy" stores in the United States. Brand names such as Lipton and A&P helped to bridge the growing divide between industrial manufacturers and ordinary consumers. By the turn of the century, H. J. Heinz was devising endless advertising gimmicks – ranging from miniature pickle pins to an Atlantic City pleasure pier – to increase sales of his "57 varieties" of canned foods. The National Biscuit Company likewise devoted a lavish promotional campaign to its "Uneeda" cracker. Competitors with equally silly brand names but without comparable advertising budgets failed to dent Nabisco's market share. Hence, the huge investments in factories and distribution required equally massive publicity to ensure demand for processed foods.

## New foods

The industrial revolution not only applied novel methods for food preparation but also created entirely new foods. Haphazard experiments with plant and animal breeding had made agriculture possible in the Neolithic age, but scientific advances of the nineteenth century radically accelerated the rate of change. By deciphering the basic properties of foods, chemists developed additives to slow decay and artificial substitutes for naturally occurring products. Improved understanding of genetics allowed biologists to create hybrids specifically accommodated to the demands of industrialization. Although food science started out as a result of shortages in fresh produce, it soon encompassed the domestic art of cooking, moving work from the home to the factory.

The modern edible oil industry arose in response to the difficulty of supplying fresh dairy to urban dwellers. An 1866 competition sponsored by the French government to find a fat substitute for the military and the working classes inspired chemist Hipolyte Mège-Mouriés to adapt the age-old technology of churning butter to other substances. Called "oleomargarine," the new product comprised emulsified beef tallow, skimmed milk, water, and salt for flavoring. As inexpensive margarine gained widespread use, dairy farmers lobbied to prevent manufacturers from dyeing their product yellow and thus confusing it with butter. Compound lard, a similar mixture of cottonseed oil and tallow, became the standard cooking medium for the fish and chip shops that first opened in London and Lancashire in the 1860s. Scientists later discovered hydrogenation, saturating vegetable oils with hydrogen, in order to achieve a solid consistency.

In the United States, a seemingly endless stream of novelties began migrating from food science laboratories to home kitchens. Gail Borden responded to the demand for less perishable milk by developing canned condensed milk in the 1850s, although it was nearly fifty years later that the Campbell's Soup

Company devised a similar technique for making condensed soup to solve the marketing problem of bulky cans. The opening of California's "bonanza farms" in the 1880s and 1890s provided abundant fruits and vegetables, but even with refrigerated railroad cars, fresh greens could rarely survive the transcontinental passage until the invention, in 1903, of the virtually indestructible iceberg lettuce. After 1920, hand-baked breads fell victim to the standardized, mass-produced, and pre-sliced Wonder Bread.

In the case of breakfast cereals, technology significantly altered the way people ate by replacing hot morning porridges with cold convenience foods. Dr. John Harvey Kellogg, director of a Seventh Day Adventist Sanitarium in Battle Creek, Michigan, created corn flakes around 1900 as a cure for patients. Kellogg's brother William soon began marketing this new food to the public, while former Battle Creek patient Charles A. Post founded a rival company selling a cereal beverage, Postum. Although cold cereals replaced hot porridge as the standard breakfast food throughout much of the country, stone-ground corn grits remained the daily staple in the South. Such resistance to mass-produced foods became increasingly common as industry extended its global reach.

## New worries

At the turn of the twentieth century, concern that industrialization would lead to social upheaval provoked a progressive reform movement on both sides of the Atlantic. Middle-class reformers feared both the growing proletariat and the unchecked power of corporations. The resulting consumer movements, heirs to the moral economy of eighteenth-century food rioters, sought to mobilize political support for government regulation of the marketplace.

The safety of packaged foods inspired some of the most visceral reactions against industrial capitalism. Widespread accounts of fraud and adulteration led the New York *Evening Post* to parody:

> Mary had a little lamb,
> And when she saw it sicken,
> She shipped it off to Packingtown,
> And now it's labeled chicken.

Even more troubling were the standard practices of treating foods with chemical additives and preservatives that had unknown health effects. Canned foods contained copper and tin, diverse metal alloys were used to color children's confectionery, and cheese was mixed with lead and mercury salts. The meatpacking industry routinely employed substantial quantities of borax and boracic acid, antiseptic compounds originally used to treat wounds, in order to convey "meat, hams, bacon, etc., from very distant places to market in a perfectly sweet and fresh state."

Health issues aside, consumers often resisted the changes to their foods caused by industrialization. Although invented in France, canned foods had little appeal to local workers, who preferred the taste of fresh meat and vegetables. Gaining widespread acceptance required more than a century of educational efforts both through domestic hygiene classes to inform French women about the benefits of canning and by military commissaries to inculcate a taste for canned food among French men. Refrigerated meats also underwent considerable change in taste during transportation. In the United States, the giant meatpackers used their cost advantage to drive out competitors offering freshly slaughtered beef, except for kosher butchers supplying Jewish immigrants in New York City. In London markets, fresh beef commanded a substantial premium over chilled and frozen meat until the upheavals around World War I caused a complete transition in the supply chain from livestock to refrigerated meat. Although mass-produced foods eventually supplanted other sources of supply, this change came over the objections of many consumers.

Progressive reformers soon grew concerned about the concentration of economic power in the hands of giant corporations. Nineteenth-century liberalism had embraced free trade as the best guarantee of public well-being, yet the ability of meatpackers, for example, to crush independent butchers challenged this belief. The massive investments required for modern industry promoted not open competition between numerous buyers and sellers but rather cooperation between a few dominant firms. Food processing companies integrated their operations through industrial trusts such as the National Packing Company, the American Sugar and Refining Company, and the United Fruit Company. Yet what "captains of industry" perceived as beneficial oligopolies raised public fears of monopolistic profiteering by "robber barons." The Interstate Commerce Act (1887) and the Sherman Anti-Trust Act (1890) sought to prevent such industrial collusion, although prosecutors often found it difficult to prove monopolistic practices in court.

Women also took the initiative in progressive politics, particularly through the home economics movement. Modern feminists have lamented the unequal gender roles defined by Catherine Beecher's *Treatise on Domestic Economy* (1841), but turn-of-the-century reformers sought to translate maternal roles into political influence outside the home. Ellen Richards, the first woman graduate from MIT (1873), saw scientific training as an avenue for professional careers. Home economics teachers sought practical solutions to problems such as adulterated foods. Middle-class, often religiously oriented women's groups strongly advocated government health inspection and proved crucial allies of Dr. Harvey Wiley, chief chemist of the U.S. Department of Agriculture, in his campaign for a federal Food and Drug Act. Unfortunately, the concern for scientific legitimacy often led home economists to pursue efficiency at the expense of palatability. In 1890, for example, Richards helped establish the New England Kitchen to teach poor Boston women how to prepare boiled dinners and Indian pudding, but the demonstration kitchen soon closed due to lack of interest by immigrants who preferred ethnic foods to bland Yankee fare.

Securing pure food legislation represented one of the great triumphs of the progressive movement. Municipal health boards, whose sanitary responsibilities included food inspection, had already been founded throughout Europe and North America by the middle of the nineteenth century. During an era of free trade, these local bodies often struggled to assert legal jurisdiction, and inspection was all the more difficult for foods canned in distant factories. Britain pioneered a national regulatory system with a series of Adulteration Acts in the 1870s. Following international health conferences, both Canada and Australia passed laws in 1905 prohibiting the adulteration of food. The publication of Upton Sinclair's muckraking novel *The Jungle* (1906), which graphically depicted unsanitary conditions in Chicago packinghouses, finally assured action by the U.S. Congress to require the inspection of foods sold in interstate commerce. Because these early laws did not always define just what should be in particular foods, prosecutors were hard pressed, once again, to prove adulteration. Nevertheless, progressive legislation took an important step forward by reasserting government responsibility for consumer protection.

## Conclusion

The industrialization of food dramatically transformed the livelihoods of people in Europe and North America in the nineteenth century and throughout the world in the twentieth century. As standards of living began to rise, commoners gained access to luxury foods. Hunger and anemia were no longer the inevitable lot of the working class, but improved access to meat, fats, and sugars brought heart disease, diabetes, and obesity to ever greater numbers. Advances in food science made it possible to eat more refined foods, but at the expense of a growing sense of alienation, as home cooking was replaced by factory labor. The widening scope of consumerism brought a ceaseless barrage of advertising, creating new demands as an ever more wasteful disposable society emerged.

Progressive responses to the challenge of industrialization likewise had ambivalent effects, particularly in the United States. The Pure Food and Drug Act allowed giant firms to eliminate smaller competitors, who could not afford the added expenses of inspection. Home economists meanwhile began to work for the food industry, using their seemingly impartial educational mission as advertising for brand name foods and appliances. Even the outcry against supposedly dangerous products often concealed xenophobic motives. Industries dominated by native Anglo businessmen, including milling and cereal manufacturing, soft drinks, and fast food, met with little progressive opposition. On the other hand, breweries, wineries, and meatpacking firms – with prominent German, Irish, Italian, and Eastern European owners – inspired muckraking and prohibitionist outrage. As the nation came to be associated with industrial foods at the dawn of the twentieth century, the origins of those foods provoked intense controversies. Other nations likewise paid close attention to the cuisines that helped to shape their collective identities.

## Further reading

On the industrialization of food, see Jack Goody, *Cooking, Cuisine and Class: A Study in Comparative Sociology* (Cambridge: Cambridge University Press, 1982); Harvey A. Levenstein, *Revolution at the Table: The Transformation of the American Diet* (New York: Oxford University Press, 1988); William Cronon, *Nature's Metropolis: Chicago and the Great West* (New York: W. W. Norton, 1991); and Roger Horowitz, *Meat in America: Technology, Taste, Transformation* (Baltimore, MD: Johns Hopkins University Press, 2005). On consumer reactions, see Martin Breugel, "How the French Learned to Eat Canned Food, 1809–1930s," and Donna R. Gabaccia, "As American as Budweiser and Pickles? Nation-Building in American Food Industries," both in Warren Belasco and Philip Scranton (eds), *Food Nations: Selling Taste in Consumer Societies* (New York: Routledge, 2002); James Harvey Young, *Pure Food: Securing the Federal Food and Drugs Act of 1906* (Princeton, NJ: Princeton University Press, 1989); and Lorine Swainston Goodwin, *The Pure Food, Drink, and Drug Crusaders, 1879–1914* (Jefferson, NC: McFarland & Co., 1999).

# Chapter 7

# Cuisine and nation-building

The rise of nation states has been the dominant political trend in modern world history. Although a patriotic love of homeland reaches back to the ancient world, the sense of nations as communities of people sharing a common culture and history appeared only in the eighteenth century. Nationalism was the ideological belief that the nation, however defined, had a right to self-government as a sovereign state. In practice, nationalist movements emerged not in political vacuums but rather as attempts to seize power from kings or empires ruling over multi-ethnic peoples. In 1789, for example, Louis XVI's subjects spoke mutually unintelligible dialects, practiced distinct customs, and worshipped different faiths. Nationalist leaders in France, as elsewhere, had to instill a common language, culture, and history – while suppressing regional identities – in order to gain the allegiance of the people they claimed to represent.

No single logic explains the diversity of nationalist movements, and there have been at least three waves of nation-building since the mid-eighteenth century. The first nationalists, in the Americas and Western Europe, invented the language of popular sovereignty to justify the power they gained resisting absolutist monarchs. A second rank of nations coalesced in the mid-nineteenth century in response to threats by nationalist aggressors, particularly the Napoleonic invasion of Europe. These new communities often resulted from the clash of rival nationalist movements representing elite projects and popular uprisings, with Bismarck's Germany and Meiji Japan tending toward the former and the latter exemplified by the Italian Risorgimento and Czech resistance to Austrian and Prussian domination. Finally, the mid-twentieth-century dissolution of European empires conceived an even more prolific nationalist generation in Africa and Asia.

Nationalist champions often claim ancient lineages and quasi-mythical origins, but the tools and goals of nation-building are distinctly modern. Universal schooling in the language of the metropolis not only functioned to unify regional dialects but also provided a vital foundation for industrial society. Compulsory military service likewise drilled patriotism into the masses while asserting national power. In the twentieth century, mass media and even sporting events have become vital instruments for constructing national identities, and of all cultural symbols, few have such deep affective roots as childhood foods.

But just as nations have been described as "imagined communities," one could question whether national cuisines exist except as artificial collections of foods eaten by people living within arbitrary political boundaries. Culinary practices invariably differ from one region to the next, so for national cuisines to exist at all, they must likewise be imagined from diverse local foods. This act of cultural creation, which paralleled the larger process of nation-building, occurred first in France.

## French gastronomy

Having replaced the monarchy with a national government, the French Revolution of 1789 also brought about the nationalization of Versailles's court cuisine. Legend has it that this transformation came about when chefs of the aristocracy were left unemployed by the guillotine and began catering to the masses by opening restaurants. In fact, an entirely new cultural field, gastronomy, emerged to codify rules for proper eating, in effect translating court rituals for the bourgeoisie. The most genial of gastronomes, Anthelme Brillat-Savarin, insisted: "Animals feed; man eats; only the intelligent man knows how to eat." This emphasis on individual taste rejected the old regime ranking by birth while creating new social distinctions, based on knowledge and wealth, rather than genuine democracy. Moreover, a widespread belief in the superiority of French cuisine garnered premium prices for wine and food exports as well as lucrative positions for French chefs. Yet the hegemony of Parisian gastronomy did not go unchallenged, either by foreign nationalists or in the provinces of France.

French culinary discourse, based on the consumption of texts as well as foods, took shape in the early nineteenth century. Alexandre Grimod de la Reynière, a former aristocrat renowned for extravagance, pioneered culinary journalism with his popular *Gourmands' Almanac* (1803–12), which directed readers to the finest restaurants and food suppliers. Cookbooks by chef Antonin Carême meanwhile professionalized the kitchen, simplifying and systematizing haute cuisine to make it more accessible. Finally, Brillat-Savarin's witty *Physiology of Taste* (1826) made reading about food as pleasurable as eating. Professionals notwithstanding, gastronomy also depended for its influence on non-specialist writings such as the novels of Honoré de Balzac set in Parisian restaurants.

Gastronomy, like French nationality, was theoretically open to all, but required the assimilation of a distinctively Parisian culture. Although few could afford truffles and rare wine, Brillat-Savarin suggested tests of gastronomy accommodated to every budget. "My book is not written for great houses alone," Carême likewise insisted. "I would like every citizen in our beautiful France to be able to eat delicious food." Nevertheless, cookbooks employed a specialized and self-referential language of honorific titles (maître d'butter) and historic names (Soubise sauce). Parisian whimsy also revised geography; pheasant *à la Périgord* at least paid homage to regional ingredients, truffles, but fish dumplings *à la Lyonnaise* bore little resemblance to provincial cooking. Chefs even conferred French nationality on such foreign dishes as Hollandaise sauce and English turtle soup.

The restaurant menu provided a crucial intersection between text and practice in this modern gastronomic culture. In the eighteenth century, *restaurants* had been restorative broths intended for personal ailments; eventually restaurateurs came to offer full meals, but as distinct individual servings, unlike the shared platters of aristocratic banquets or common inns. These establishments also straddled the boundary between public and private, with chambers available for more than culinary pleasures. Nineteenth-century restaurants were thus uniquely Parisian institutions, and simply ordering a meal required a high degree of literacy in the new idiom. Dining degenerated into social combat, a struggle to maintain status and avoid humiliation by waiters who announced in menacing jargon: "Your brains are being fried; I'll bring you your tongue, the chef is going to cut off your head."

Even the Parisian working classes shared in this new culinary culture through the spread of cafés. Condemned by moralists as the haunts of drunken men and disreputable women, cafés actually became a place for workers to socialize and for families to spend a quiet evening; Balzac described them as the "parliament of the people." The food and wine did not meet the standards of exclusive restaurants, but it was still far more varied and plentiful in the mid-nineteenth century thanks to railroad transportation. Parisian workers were veritable gourmets in comparison with meager peasant diets, although many bistros recycled leftovers from wealthier tables. Consumption also differed widely between well-paid artisans and itinerant laborers.

The project of nation-building, like the creation of Parisian gastronomy, involved forging a unified French identity at the expense of regional loyalties, but peasants insisted on negotiating the terms of their incorporation into the national community. Champagne, for example, gained recognition through clever marketing as the most "French" of all wines and as a celebratory drink the world over. Producers ensured exclusivity by cultivating a mystique of *terroir*, referring to the particular soil, climate, and even soul of the winemaker. By French law, only sparkling wine from the region of Champagne could carry the coveted appellation. Yet the meaning of *terroir* became problematic when industrial firms such as Moët & Chandon began importing grapes from outside the region, a practice that ended only when armed revolt by farmers in 1911 prompted new legislation requiring the use of local grapes. The growers thus asserted their own place within the nation.

The spread of French food throughout Europe caused dismay among Italian nationalists, even as Napoleon III frustrated the completion of Italy's unification until 1870. Gallic supremacy seemed all the more outrageous because

Italian chefs had been setting culinary fashions since the Renaissance. Pellegrino Artusi finally challenged Francophile cookery by publishing *Science in the Kitchen and the Art of Eating Well* (1891). Notwithstanding the positivist tone of the title, the recipes sparkled with grace and humor, gaining a wide following throughout the country. The book arguably invented an Italian national cuisine by unifying bourgeois society with regional dialects, although it remained limited to the duality of Romagnol-Bolognese richness and Tuscan simplicity, supplemented by an occasional Genovese, Sicilian, Neapolitan, or other regional dish. Many lands outside of Europe were also undergoing the process of nation-building at this time, and they shared the same ideals and dilemmas of Italian culinary nation-building.

## Latin America

Latin Americans took the lead in imagining distinctive national identities but paradoxically lagged behind in achieving national unification. American-born Creoles, subordinated by imperial policy to peninsular Spaniards, had already begun to develop a sense of patriotism opposed to the Spanish crown by the mid-eighteenth century. Nevertheless, colonial social conflicts between wealthy creoles and indigenous and racially mixed masses destabilized newly independent governments after 1820. The lower classes particularly resisted elite attempts at social engineering designed to build European-style industrial nations by transforming their agrarian lifestyle and popular culture. Not until the early twentieth century did models of nationhood, including national cuisines, take root in local conditions rather than European ideals.

Creole elites clung to European culture, even while proclaiming the wisdom of dead Aztec and Inca kings, in order to distinguish themselves from contemporary Indians, who were at the bottom of the social pyramid. Iberian styles predominated until independence, but over the nineteenth century, French culture came into fashion. Thus, Mexican cookbooks gradually replaced Spanish mutton stew with *bifstec à la Chateaubriand*, while excluding Native American tamales as the food of "the lower orders." At the 1910 independence celebrations, not a single Mexican dish appeared in a score of French banquets dedicated to the patriotic occasion. Wealthy Chileans profited from their own continental sophistication by exporting fine wines made with grapes from Bordeaux rootstock. Deliberately calculated to exclude the unsophisticated, French cuisine was an obvious choice for Latin American elites anxious to demonstrate their superiority by hobnobbing at exclusive restaurants. Moreover, they attended these dinners dressed in worsted wool frockcoats and top hats more appropriate to foggy London than to tropical Rio de Janeiro. The infatuation with European culture reached such heights that during a controversy over the sale of property to a foreigner, one Chilean wit suggested: "Why don't we sell the entire country to France and buy ourselves something smaller, close to Paris?"

Even as Latin American elites mimicked the *haute bourgeoisie*, a nutritional discourse emerged to explain the failure of national development. José Ramón López composed a treatise, *Food and the Races* (1896), arguing that the Caribbean diet based on plantains lacked the nutritional value needed for the Dominican Republic to become modern. In Mexico, Francisco Bulnes concluded that "the [European] race of wheat is the only truly progressive one," and that "maize has been the eternal pacifier of America's indigenous races and the foundation of their refusal to become civilized." While using dubious nutritional calculations, these positivist intellectuals at least sought scientific explanations based on culture rather than social Darwinist genetic determinism. Moreover, peasants able to support themselves with sturdy crops like maize or plantains had little incentive to submit to the exploitation of early industrialization.

Beginning around World War I, *fin-de-siècle* Francophiles lost power to a new generation of populists demanding universal rights of citizenship. In Mexico, the invention of mechanical tortilla factories commoditized the formerly subsistence agriculture, drawing peasants into the national economy, while an indigenous nationalism enshrined enchiladas and tamales at the heart of the national cuisine. Brazilians of the 1930s likewise celebrated African and Native American influences – symbolic of their supposed "racial democracy" – in the rice and black beans of *feijoada*. French cuisine also began to fade from public banquets in Buenos Aires, Lima, and Santiago, increasingly replaced by Creole specialties, the abundant roast meats of Argentine *churrasco*, the fresh seafood of Peruvian *ceviche*, and the chicken, corn, and olives of Chilean *pastel de choclo*. Thus, the Latin American acceptance of European cultural superiority, instilled through centuries of colonial rule, was finally balanced by a rediscovery of local values. In Asia, by contrast, the encounter with Western modernity came more abruptly and resulted in more variable experiences of nation-building.

## Asia

Nationalism, like Western technology and culture, posed dilemmas for Asian societies. Mobilizing the masses offered a potential response to European incursions, but at the risk of undermining traditions of order and deference. Traumatized by the mid-nineteenth-century Opium Wars and the Taiping Rebellion, China's Qing dynasty equivocated in adopting Western practices until its downfall in 1911. By contrast, Commodore Perry's opening of Japan in 1853 led to a strictly controlled process of Westernization. Reformers launched a program of social engineering, including dietary reform, to focus nationalist sentiment on the restored emperor Meiji (ruled 1868–1912). The kingdom of Siam meanwhile preserved its sovereignty as a buffer state between rival European powers, thereby limiting the social disruptions of Westernization. The role of food in modernization differed in each case according to customary social values.

With its ancient and resilient civilization, China viewed modern nationalism with ambivalence. Foreign foodstuffs had long been incorporated into established culinary repertoires, while novel kitchen practices were rejected as barbarous. "Judge now what tastes people possess who sit at table and swallow bowls of a fluid, in their outlandish tongue called *Soo-pe*," William Hunter parodied Chinese reactions to Western cooking. "Dishes of half-raw meat are then placed at various angles of the table; these float in gravy, while from them pieces are cut with swordlike instruments." Nationalist leader Sun Yatsen assailed the Qing dynasty as ethnically distinct from the Han majority, but Manchu rulers still ate Chinese court cuisine. This confusion of culture and ethnic origin, together with the impracticality of nationalizing Mandarin practices to the peasant masses, meant cuisine contributed little positive to China's revolutions. Nationalist military conquests of the 1920s resembled nothing so much as the unifying accession of a short-lived dynasty. The Maoist regime later sought to standardize language and education, a process ironically akin to nationalization, while purging extravagant banquets – essentially trading a cuisine for a nation.

Unlike China, Japan had a long history of adopting foreign culture, notwithstanding Tokugawa-era isolation. Meiji reformers, determined to avoid the Qing fate, decreed compulsory schooling aimed at building a strong, Westernized nation. Along with industrial and military technology, the Japanese avidly adopted British beef. Buddhist piety had long proscribed the slaughter and consumption of four-legged animals, and early proponents of Western food and manners earned the epithet *bataa-kusai* (butter stinkers). This initial aversion relented as news spread in 1872 that the Emperor had eaten beef. Military rations also included beef to inculcate the taste among conscripts. Numerous Western restaurants sprang up in cities, although a Japanese-style stew, *sukiyaki*, ultimately became the favorite cooking method. The extent of Westernization was limited at first; the major change in rural consumption in the late nineteenth century was greater consumption of white rice, soy sauce, and other "traditional" Japanese dishes. Even in cities, beef did not replace indigenous foods nor supplant the ritual importance of rice. Indeed, rice became a primary focus of official nationalism, in opposition to beef, notwithstanding the instrumental role of Western diet in economic development.

The kingdom of Siam responded with diplomacy rather than militarism to preserve independence from Western powers. Chulalongkorn (ruled 1868–1910) followed an almost colonial modernization program of centralizing power and building infrastructure rather than nationalist education. Nevertheless, the combination of Indian curries, Chinese noodles, and Thai flavors – coriander, garlic, and black (later chile) pepper – was shared by both court and commoners alike, differing primarily in variety and degree of ornamentation. Indeed, the long-ruling king enjoyed the rustic foods of his subjects, "rice in a blackened pot; on coconut shell dishes, fried lettuce, salt fish and chillie sauce." The incipient Thai national cuisine was elaborated under his successor, Wachirawut (ruled 1910–25), who directed his nationalism to an elite audience. The role of cuisine in Asian nation-building therefore followed strikingly different patterns as rulers determined what elements of Western culture fit best with local traditions.

## Conclusion

The emergence of national cuisines in some areas but not in others reflected social and political conditions rather than any objective culinary superiority. Both France and China had elaborate court cuisines, but only in the former case was it nationalized beyond a narrow elite. The British took no less pride in their beef than the French in their sauce, but these expressions of culinary nationalism did not produce comparable gastronomic cultures. Nationalist feeling may well have emerged from the sharing of common foods, but only when used in such an instrumental fashion; culinary nationalism may also be subsidiary to and later than other affiliations.

Whatever the origins, nationalism remained an ideology contested by class and region. National elites often used cultural means such as affected eating habits to demonstrate their superiority over the working classes, in order to justify depriving them of effective citizenship. Moreover, the construction of national cuisines and identities necessarily compressed the richness of regional cultures. Thus, urban elites appropriated peasant foods while modifying them greatly, not least by consuming on a daily basis what were rare festival dishes. This process of claiming a folkloric view of the people formed part of the larger mythical roots of the nationalist imagination.

Nationalist ideology also became a justification for the construction of empires. The civilizing mission that sought to instill metropolitan culture in provincial peasants extended to supposed "savages" living on distant continents. The expansion of European empires in turn deprived countless people of the ability to forge their own approaches to modernity, whether as nations or in other forms of society.

## Further reading

On Europe, Priscilla Parkhurst Ferguson, *Accounting for Taste: The Triumph of French Cuisine* (Chicago: University of Chicago Press, 2004); Rebecca L. Spang, *The Invention of the Restaurant: Paris and Modern Gastronomic Culture* (Cambridge, MA: Harvard University Press, 2000); W. Scott Haine, *The World of the Paris Café: Sociability among the French Working Class, 1789–1914* (Baltimore, MD: Johns Hopkins University Press, 1996); Kolleen M. Guy, *When Champagne Became French: Wine and the Making of a National Identity* (Baltimore, MD: Johns Hopkins University Press, 2003); and Piero Camporesi, *The Magic Harvest: Food, Folklore and Society*, trans. Joan Krakover Hall (Cambridge: Polity Press, 1993). On Latin America, Jeffrey M. Pilcher, *¡Que vivan los tamales! Food and the Making of Mexican Identity* (Albuquerque, NM:

University of New Mexico Press, 1998); and Arnold J. Bauer, *Goods, Power, History: Latin America's Material Culture* (Cambridge: Cambridge University Press, 2001). For Asia, Jonathan Spence, "Ch'ing," in K. C. Chang (ed.), *Food in Chinese Culture: Anthropological and Historical Perspectives* (New Haven, CT: Yale University Press, 1977); Emiko Ohnuki-Tierney, *Rice as Self: Japanese Identities through Time* (Princeton, NJ: Princeton University Press, 1993); Naomichi Ishige, *The History and Culture of Japanese Food* (London: Kegan Paul, 2001); and Penny Van Esterik, "From Marco Polo to McDonald's: Thai Cuisine in Transition," *Food and Foodways* 5(2) (1992): 177–93.

# Chapter 8

# Empires of food

In the second half of the nineteenth century, European nations competed to colonize the remaining independent lands of Asia and Africa. Although motivated by imperial power and prestige, colonists justified their brutal conquests with claims of uplifting "savage" peoples, a task dubbed the "White Man's Burden" by Rudyard Kipling or the *mission civilisatrice* in French. This "civilizing" ideology extended to non-western foods, which were judged inferior to European diets in both nutritional value and hygienic preparation. Frenchman J. A. Colombani wrote: "We have the responsibility to lead the peoples of overseas territory to political and social maturity, to integrate them, to imbue them with our civilization. *And is not bread the typical food of civilized people?*" But unlike modern technology and social practices, generally transmitted from Europe to the colonies, culinary exchanges often reversed the direction of influence, as the British began eating Indian rice and curry while the French acquired a taste for Algerian couscous.

As an economic undertaking, imperialism left a complicated balance sheet that historians still debate. Notwithstanding the personal fortunes accumulated by the likes of diamond magnate Cecil Rhodes and palm oil merchant Victor Régis, colonial businesses often failed to justify the expense of military occupation. Metropolitan authorities therefore insisted that the inhabitants of colonies and protectorates pay for the "protection" that was imposed upon them. Under the new international division of labor, Africans and Asians were dragooned to work on plantations and mines, supplying raw materials to European factories. However meager the wages paid, the commercialization of formerly subsistence economies had a significant impact on colonial diets. Cans of deviled ham and condensed milk turned up in the most remote villages, but occasional novelties did little to offset the nutritional harm caused by the diversion of farmland to coffee, tea, and other export crops. To compensate for the loss of land and labor to imperial enterprises, colonial subjects were often forced to adopt unfamiliar foods from the Americas in place of traditional staples.

As a continuation of the Columbian Exchange, nineteenth-century colonialism produced diverse culinary encounters that defy easy generalization. This chapter will examine two sets of comparisons, British and French imperialists and their interactions with West African and South and South-east Asian peoples. As an initial hypothesis, one might suppose that the common imperial goal of extracting wealth from dependent territories outweighed any differences between the British and French, both in their cuisines and in their attitudes toward colonized peoples. Yet one should not focus on the rulers alone, and a second hypothesis suggests that Asians and Africans responded in different ways to the impositions of imperial power based on their existing culinary cultures. Further research is needed to provide definitive conclusions about the dietary effects of empire.

## Asia

Indian Ocean outposts, established in the sixteenth century to control the spice trade, provided a staging point for the territorial domination of Asia. Starting with the Seven Years' War (1756–1763), the British East India Company extended its authority over much of the subcontinent, and the first Opium War (1839–1842) guaranteed access to trade with China. The Indian Rebellion of 1857, led by native troops, called sepoys, who turned on their British officers, prompted the Crown to assume direct colonial rule. At about the same time, the French emperor Napoleon III launched an invasion of Indochina. Beginning with a foothold around Saigon, the French eventually carved out an Asian empire reaching from Hanoi in the north through Laos to Cambodia.

In the early years of the British East India Company, resident merchants were called nabobs because of the local habits they acquired, but Anglo sahibs of the late nineteenth century felt duty bound to maintain the prestige of imperial culture. Little dietary adjustment had been needed at first; the heavily spiced dishes of early seventeenth-century British cooking still resembled Indian stews, except for the beef and pork. Even at the height of the Raj, Anglo-Indians commonly ate curry and rice as an informal brunch, but for afternoon tea they observed Victorian rituals. The evening meal likewise followed a strictly British menu of soup, entrée, roast meat, savory pudding, and sweets, washed down with claret or beer. Dinner jackets and evening gowns – or the martial ceremonies of the regimental mess – also helped keep upper lips stiff in the tropics, although the British colonial administrator, George Atkinson conceded that "these grand spreads are cruelly ponderous, and indigestible."

Maintaining British standards of civilization in remote colonial outposts required more than just a vigorous constitution. Imperial officials employed numerous domestic servants, far more than they could have afforded at home, which made supervising the staff an important task for the *memsahib*, or Anglo-Indian lady. Cookbooks recommended daily inspections to ensure cleanliness, for Britons believed Indians to be completely lacking in hygiene, despite their concern for ritual purity. Indeed, setting an example of proper European domesticity for servants was considered an essential foundation of imperial rule. Nevertheless, memsahibs often learned to leave well enough alone in the kitchen if they found a "mug cook" who could prepare British foods.

Even as agents of empire sought to instill metropolitan culture in colonial backwaters, Indian memorabilia gained popularity in Victorian London as everyday reminders of the vast Britannic realm. Mulligatawny soup appeared on the menus of elite clubs and then spread to the middle and lower classes. Chutneys and exotic pickles supplemented the traditional preserves of British housewives, while curry provided a useful method of recycling leftovers, thereby becoming associated with the lower classes. As an ironic result of this fashion, colonial service retirees were sought after for their expertise on authentic Indian cuisine, although many had scorned it while stationed abroad. British demand also spurred the development of colonial food processing industries, including curry powders and chutneys with brand names redolent of imperial authority like Colonel Skinner and Major Grey. Such exports often bore little resemblance to Indian cooking, but locals soon adapted manufacturing techniques to their own foods; for example, A. B. Sircar, a return migrant from the United States, founded the Bengal Preserving Company about the turn of the century.

Hindu, and to a lesser degree Muslim, dietary restrictions limited colonial influences on the Indian diet. After all, the British national dish, roast beef, required the sacrifice of a sacred cow. The British Army learned the dangers of religious insensitivity when it issued Enfield rifles to sepoy troops – the order to bite open cartridges sealed with animal fat violated taboos against consuming both beef and pork and helped spark the rebellion of 1857. Hindu elites refused even to eat with the British for fear of caste pollution, a galling reversal of imperial status. About 1840, a group of radicals called Young Bengal publicly consumed beef and brandy as a rejection of Hindu traditions, but such displays represented generational struggles more than attitudes on colonial rule. The Indian home was considered a particularly sheltered site, where women were charged with maintaining family purity, even as men began experimenting with tea and other British foods. Yet travel to the imperial capital, rather than corrupting Indians, often strengthened their religious beliefs. Mahatma Gandhi, who had tasted beef in his native Gujarat, came to see vegetarianism as a moral conviction rather than simply a cultural duty while studying in London around 1890.

For the Indian population at large, colonialism entailed considerable dietary change. British authorities encouraged the diffusion of the American staples maize and potatoes in order to export wheat back to the metropolis. Such common dishes as *gobi aloo* (banquet potatoes with cauliflower) and *makki-di-roti* (corn flat bread) therefore only became widespread in the nineteenth century. The British also began planting tea in India, using Burmese workers at first, as a colonial replacement for Chinese supplies. The diversion of land from village subsistence to export-oriented plantations caused hardship not only in the subcontinent but also throughout Indochina.

The cuisine of Vietnam, like its written language and religious beliefs, developed under the tutelage of China, which ruled the country for a thousand years. The Vietnamese adopted many Chinese culinary techniques, including stir-frying, noodle making, and eating with chopsticks, but they also preserved distinctive tastes such as a preference for uncooked herbs and vegetables and a greater reliance on fermented fish sauce than on soy sauce. Regional cooking styles emerged over time, with simpler, meatier dishes prevalent in the north, while more curries, spices, and seafood were eaten in the south. The imperial capital of Hue, in the center, produced the most elaborate cuisine: small, intricately worked delicacies reminiscent of Thai court foods.

French colonists in Vietnam, even more than Anglo-Indian sahibs, insisted on having access to familiar foods, although the climate still required many adjustments. Those traditional custodians of French civilization, bakers, responded creatively to wheat shortages by extending their dough with rice flour. Cafés, butcher shops, and sausage makers also flourished along the newly constructed boulevards of Saigon and Hanoi. The French introduced many garden plants, particularly asparagus, which the Vietnamese called Western bamboo, and when local crops failed to meet demand, they imported canned asparagus from France. Many Vietnamese adopted the culture of their rulers; the urbane Phoung Do Huu, for example, gained the respect of French colonists for his splendid table, but culinary blending took place in even the most Francophile homes. Native ingredients transformed many dishes, such as crème caramel and ice cream made with coconut milk. Moreover, the Vietnamese were as likely to dip their baguette in curry as to eat it with pâté. Even canned imports from Europe acquired a uniquely colonial flavor, as in the condensed milk of Vietnamese *café au lait*.

The kitchen could become the site of colonial resistance as well as collaboration. The northern Vietnamese breakfast soup, *pho*, made with rice noodles and thin slices of beefsteak cooked rare in the French style, was often linked to the similar sounding Gallic *pot-au-feu*. More patriotic writers of the 1930s rejected this imperial genealogy and embraced *pho* as a nationalist symbol, ironically tracing its origins back to an earlier invasion, by the Mongols, who supposedly introduced their hotpots to Vietnam in the fourteenth century. Such political consciousness-raising also took place in middle-class cookbooks, which carried advertisements for anti-colonial publications.

Peasants in the countryside had little opportunity to sample French delicacies; many could scarcely afford to eat rice as the colonial regime expanded its agricultural exports. Although not traditionally a significant part of the French diet, rice pilaf became more common on metropolitan tables over the course of the nineteenth century. The resulting expansion of the Vietnamese commercial economy forced peasants to sell their rice harvest, subsisting instead on maize and sweet potatoes. Coffee, tea, and rubber plantations also became widespread, but perhaps the most hated symbol of the colonial presence was the alcohol monopoly. The French not only imposed village quotas for the purchase of industrial distilled drinks but also searched native households for illicit alcohol.

The process of culinary exchange in colonial Asia varied considerably among the elite, who could pick and choose from foreign menus, but the dietary practices of the masses were determined more heavily by imperial economic calculations. On the whole, the British tended to take more from and give less to India, while French cuisine had a greater attraction to wealthy Vietnamese than vice versa. Indian dietary restrictions, the historical openness of Vietnam to Chinese influence, and the nineteenth-century British infatuation with French haute cuisine may all have contributed to this outcome. Nevertheless, for European colonists and prominent Asians alike, cross-cultural adaptation took place at the margins, most often at breakfast or dessert. By contrast, the disruptions to peasant food habits tended to strike at the heart of their diets, a pattern that was even more exaggerated in African colonies.

## Africa

Trade led the imperial flag in Africa as in Asia, starting from commercial posts established since the fifteenth century. With the British abolition of the slave trade in 1807, merchants turned to agricultural exports, especially palm oil and peanuts. European explorers and missionaries began charting the interior by the 1830s, although the division of African lands took place only in the 1880s. The French advanced from bases in Algeria and Senegal to claim the bulk of West Africa, even as the British seized a north–south axis ranging from Egypt to South Africa. Tiny Belgium acquired an enormous colony in the Congo, while Portugal expanded long-held outposts in Angola and Mozambique. Finally, Germany and Italy gathered up scattered territories left over by other powers. By 1900, only the kingdom of Ethiopia had success-fully defended its independence. Nevertheless, the physical occupation of the continent proceeded more slowly because of the difficulty of communications and railroad building. Not until the 1930s did Europeans assert a measure of control over the vast spaces that had been marked out fifty years earlier on colonial maps.

Although the solitary explorer, with pith helmet and hunting rifle, has become a common western image of Africa, colonial mythology neglects the long train of native porters who provided travelers with canned meat and biscuits, bottles of beer, wine, and Vichy water, and other staples of European civilization. Captain Jean-Baptiste Marchand brought cases of champagne all the way from the Congo to Fashoda in 1898, but the French celebration was cut short when Lord Kitchener claimed Sudan for Britain. The desire for familiar food notwithstanding, Europeans also enjoyed shooting big game and frequently debated the gastronomic merits of zebra, hippopota-mus, and crocodile. Mary Kingsley declared that "a good snake, properly cooked, is one of the best meats one gets out here." Not surprisingly, colonists acquired a reputation for profligacy among Africans, who often consumed a single daily meal. In the 1930s, British anthropologist Audrey Richards overheard one Bantu youth inform his playmates: "You know nothing about Europeans! That is just what they do all day – just sit and call, 'Boy! Bring me food.'"

Feeding Europeans, both locally and through agricultural exports, dramatically transformed the African ecology. The fragile nature of the soil had prompted the development of highly complex agricultural systems. In Nigeria, for example, Igbo farmers intercropped numerous varieties of yam with taro, groundnuts, and chile peppers, thus combining native domesticates with Asian and American foods to provide a balanced diet while maintaining soil fertility and compensating for irregular rains. By contrast, colonial plantations concentrated on individual cash crops with European markets. Senegalese peanuts and Nigerian oil palms found new applications in making soap and industrial lubricants. Coffee and cacao plantations in the Gold and Ivory coasts employed irrigation and fertilizers with devastating long-term consequences for the soil.

Colonial regimes had equally dramatic effects on local social arrangements. The goal of reproducing European agricultural and industrial revolutions led to the enclosure – a euphemism for expropriation – of land and livestock. Administrators also resettled scattered hamlets into larger fixed villages, which increased the demands on marginal soils. The plantation system drew male migrant workers from the arid interior, doubling the workload of women who stayed behind. Commercialization of food production threatened communal support systems designed to spread the risks of a bad harvest. Although people traditionally shared the fruits of their farm labor among even distant family members, foods purchased with newly acquired cash were often considered exempt from such obligations, leading to increased inequality. Colonial game laws disrupted male communal hunts and deprived entire villages of an important source of protein. Admittedly, the effects of such changes varied, depending on the nature of tribal societies. The absence of male migrant workers proved less of a burden in matrilineal societies, where women could rely on relatives for support. Communities that were already well integrated into regional markets likewise faced fewer dislocations than did more isolated villages engaged in subsistence agriculture.

Missionary teachers sought to transform African eating habits to instill bourgeois Christian family values, and African culinary cultures often proved more receptive to European paternalism than did those of South Asia. In many societies, the act of feeding others created strong ties of dependency, so handouts of canned beef or an elephant brought down by hunting rifle placed servants in debt to their European employers. Non-Muslim Africans held individualized food taboos – a refusal to eat a particular food considered offensive to their personal guardian spirits – rather than more resilient communal dietary restrictions.

Nevertheless, European meals, without the traditional balance of porridge and relish, left Africans feeling hungry and unsatisfied. Missionary attempts to replace communal eating habits with a nuclear family centered on the dinner table likewise encountered resistance. As in Asia, the domestic sphere proved to be a safeguard of many traditional values. Audrey Richards concluded that African women "were far less in awe of the European than the men."

European scientific knowledge provided a cornerstone of the civilizing mission, but this ideology of racial superiority was relatively slow to recognize nutrition – an environmental rather than genetic explanation of backwardness. Tropical medicine generally focused on diseases that threatened European settlers, particularly malaria, while strictly African problems like sleeping sickness received less attention. Nutrition entered the colonial agenda when mining company officials called for better rations to improve the productivity of African workers. Even then, caloric gains usually came through the provision of carbohydrates in the convenient form of manioc and sugar, rather than programs to assure more balanced diets for entire families.

Far from passive subjects, Africans took the initiative in coping with European colonial demands. The Sine of Senegal successfully incorporated peanut exports into existing crop rotations, thus helping to preserve social networks. Igbo women and men often voluntarily concentrated their labor on palm oil exports in order to earn more cash, even when doing so meant replacing yams with more productive but less nutritious manioc. Similar dietary trade-offs were common among women forced to assume traditionally male tasks such as clearing land. Many single women turned to brewing as a regular source of income rather than as an occasional festive activity, and drunkenness increased despite colonial restrictions on alcohol. Even the adoption of European foods came on African terms; coffee, tea, and sardines, for example, were often consumed for prestige value after the daily porridge and relish had been finished rather than as part of the regular meal.

Yet the acceptance of European foods as items of prestige ultimately left a significant long-term dietary legacy. Brewing was one of the first industries to be established by Africans, and as bottled beer replaced more nutritious, freshly made brews, women lost a valuable source of cash income. European-educated colonial elites became even more convinced of the superiority of metropolitan culture. Wild greens, insects, and small animals were sacrificed as contributions to local diets, while urban markets become dependent on expensive imported wheat and rice. In the Côte d'Ivoire, for example, bakeries turned out perfect baguettes, and valuable foreign exchange was lavished on imported French cheese.

## Conclusion

The civilizing mission, although ostensibly based on objective science, reflected the European cultural bias about the superiority of their food habits. The local knowledge of indigenous farmers often proved far more productive in the long term than commercial agriculture based on irrigation and fertilizers that plundered natural resources. Nor did the adoption of modern nutritional science always ensure better health for people who consumed industrial processed foods.

Perhaps the most insidious effect of colonialism was in breaking down social mechanisms designed to ensure collective survival in difficult environments. Europeans consciously adopted a policy of divide and rule by making collaboration highly profitable on an individual basis, thereby exacerbating tribal and religious rivalries. Even native elites who worked with colonial rulers were denied equality within the European racial hierarchy. Moreover, by the twentieth century, colonial schooling was directed away from cultural assimilation toward proletarian mechanical arts.

Overall, the effects of colonialism seem to have outweighed native social structures in shaping the outcome of culinary intervention. Asian elites, with their own haute cuisines, proved more resistant to European influence than their African counterparts. But imperial exploitation had severe nutritional consequences for the lower classes of both continents. The attempts of subject peoples to accommodate the international division of labor were further undermined by the colonial diffusion of plants. The British established Indonesian palm oil plantations, for example, to compete with Nigerian produce, thereby impoverishing both societies. Yet colonialism was not the only mechanism for moving foods around the world in the late nineteenth century; proletarian labor migrations likewise contributed to the continued globalization of cuisine.

## Further reading

The seminal study of cooking under colonialism is Jack Goody, *Cooking, Cuisine and Class: A Study in Comparative Sociology* (Cambridge: Cambridge University Press, 1982). For Africa, see also Eno Blankson Ikpe, *Food and Society in Nigeria: A History of Food Customs, Food Economy and Cultural Change, 1900–1989* (Stuttgart: Franz Steiner Verlag, 1994); Diana Wylie, *Starving on a Full Stomach: Hunger and the Triumph of Cultural Racism in Modern South Africa* (Charlottesville, VA: University Press of Virginia, 2001); and Alice L. Conklin, *A Mission to Civilize: The Republican Idea of Empire in France and West Africa, 1895–1930* (Stanford, CA: Stanford University Press, 1997). On Asia, K. T. Achaya, *The Food Industries of British India* (Delhi: Oxford University Press, 1994); E. M. Collingham, *Imperial Bodies: The Physical Experience of the Raj, c. 1800–1947* (Cambridge: Polity Press, 2001); Milton E. Osborne, *The French Presence in Cochinchina and Cambodia: Rule and Response (1859–1905)* (Ithaca, NY: Cornell University Press, 1969); and David Burton, *French Colonial Cookery* (London: Faber and Faber, 2000).

# Chapter 9

# Migrant cuisines

Steamships and railroads opened a new world of mobility not only for colonial rulers but also for ordinary workers – those who actually mined the coal and laid the rails to make such travel possible. In the six decades from the Irish potato famine to World War I, more than 50 million people journeyed back and forth around the globe in search of opportunity. Of this great proletarian migration, the majority left Europe as free workers and settled in the temperate climates of North and South America and Australasia. Large numbers of Asians and Africans traveled as indentured workers, often called coolies, and became the primary source of labor for tropical plantations after the abolition of the slave trade. As the Chinese and Italian examples show, migrants overcame difficult working conditions and frequent discrimination to recreate traditional lifestyles and recipes, even while experimenting with novel foods in a display of working-class cosmopolitanism that contributed significantly to culinary globalization.

Diverse motives simultaneously pushed migrant workers away from their homelands and pulled them to new lands. China experienced widespread instability and hunger in the nineteenth century as colonial wars and domestic insurgency undermined the Qing dynasty. The struggle for Italian unification caused far less disruption, but workers suffered from international competition and the preference given to industrialists and large landowners by the new national government, established in 1861. Despite these troubles, people with the resources to migrate were seldom the most impoverished. The chief sending region from China was the prosperous Pearl River Delta, which escaped the worst ravages of the Taiping Rebellion. Merchant ships with news of gold strikes in California and Australia inspired the first fortune-hunters to leave Guangzhou (Canton). Italian migrants likewise followed the lure of better work and bread – "pane e lavoro." Thus, the pull of opportunity abroad often outweighed the push of hardship at home, and millions of sojourners later returned to their native lands to enjoy the fruits of their labor.

Migrants formed extensive social networks to compensate for the disorientation of being uprooted from their homelands. Both Chinese and Italian workers usually traveled without female relatives and had to provide domestic services such as cooking for themselves. For protection and fellowship, they sought out people from their town or region and formed mutual aid societies. Individuals who settled in a new country also used their knowledge and resources to arrange for relatives and neighbors to follow them. This pattern of "chain migration" created transnational families and communities that were connected by regular communication, money transfers, and travel across the Atlantic or Pacific Oceans. Cultural exchanges within these communities also extended to foods, which were transformed in the homelands as well as in the migrant settlements.

The experience of migration to the Americas differed widely, based on the background of workers and on the nature of the receiving society. North Americans looked with suspicion on newcomers from Southern and Eastern Europe while focusing particular racist intensity against the so-called "Yellow peril" from Asia. Italians assimilated far more easily into the multi-racial, Catholic societies of Argentina and Brazil. Chinese indentured servants labored under the worst conditions in the tropical plantations of Cuba and Peru, but by the turn of the century, they may have had more opportunities for social advancement than did their countrymen in North America. Migrants throughout the Americas sought to transplant their traditional cultures, although Chinese and Italian dishes often emerged from the new soil as barely recognizable versions of the foods of the homeland.

## Chop suey

Western images of coolie labor belie the diversity of Chinese migration patterns. Already in the eighteenth century, merchants and artisans had settled throughout South-east Asia and played an important role in satisfying the Chinese demand for pepper and other spices. In the nineteenth century, this region continued to absorb millions of Chinese migrants. Most of those who sailed to North America and Australia did so as free migrants, although they generally had to work to pay back money borrowed for the cost of the voyage. Only the smallest proportion of Chinese, perhaps fewer than 300,000, came as indentured servants to plantations in Cuba and Peru, where their plight became known as a "second slavery."

Chinese migrants encountered widespread prejudice in Australia, Canada, and the United States. Anglo settlers resented foreign competition, and racist commentary often focused on their diet: "They follow our hard-working people close on their heels, steal their trades, cheapen labor, and then sit down to a dinner of rice and potato sprouts, such as a hearty white would starve on." Many migrants eventually settled on employment in laundries and as cooks, domestic tasks considered demeaning by European men. Large numbers also worked as tenant farmers, peddling fresh vegetables up and down the Pacific Coast. Despite migrants' economic contributions, Chinatowns appeared in the popular imagination as vast opium dens. Such sentiment culminated in the Chinese Exclusion Act of 1882, which prohibited laborers from entering the United States.

Chinese migrants to Latin America started out under far worse circumstances but many eventually gained status and citizenship in their new countries. The recruitment of coolies began about the middle of the nineteenth century, as plantation owners sought new sources of captive labor following the abolition of the slave trade. Mortality was high, given wages that scarcely covered subsistence, and those who survived were generally repatriated at the end of their contracts. Nevertheless, plantation workers often gained their freedom and worked as domestics, tenant farmers, or petty traders. Although prejudice was also widespread in Latin America, particularly among the working classes who purchased groceries from Chinese shopkeepers, migrants assimilated as citizens of their new homelands. Chinese Peruvians, in particular, gained acceptance among the middle class as a counterbalance to the indigenous masses, and *chifas* (Chinese restaurants) became popular among all ranks of Peruvian society.

Wherever they traveled, Chinese sought out familiar foods, making ethnic grocery shops an important institution within the migrant community. The staple rice provided the most important import, coming from China and Hawaii until commercial cultivation began in California in the early twentieth century. Ethnic grocers also stocked a wide variety of condiments and herbal medicines, ranging from soy sauce, tofu, and ginger to bamboo shoots, dried seafood, and ginseng. Migrants even transported live fish and shellfish to stock streams and irrigation ditches, and they developed San Francisco's shrimp fishing industry before being replaced by Italian migrants in the 1880s.

The Chinese provided an indispensable source of labor in stylish restaurants and homes, but their food quickly acquired a downscale image. The first Chinese restaurants founded in San Francisco around 1850 briefly served classical banquet dishes to well-heeled Anglo patrons until anti-foreign sentiment forced the owners to retreat into ethnic enclaves. Nevertheless, Chinese chefs ran the kitchens of some of California's finest French restaurants. Migrants also turned up as chuck wagon cooks on distant ranges. Chinese-owned restaurants usually served American food to mainstream diners, although working-class customers came to appreciate inexpensive Chinese-style meals, often sold to take out. In Cuba and Peru, restaurants often had segregated menus, with Hispanic dishes listed on one side and Chinese on the other, indicating the apparent incompatibility of eastern and western cuisines. Even Chinese dishes were adapted to local tastes and ingredients; according to culinary legend, a San Francisco cook invented chop suey by throwing together leftovers for a group of hungry miners who arrived late one evening.

Subsequent generations of Chinese born in the Americas gradually began to transform popular images of their ethnic cuisine, marketing Chinatowns as exotic but intriguing tourist attractions. By the late 1920s, full-service Chinese restaurants had once more become fashionable in San Francisco and Lima, although with a narrow range of Americanized dishes. These establishments sought to overturn negative stereotypes and educate mainstream consumers about the proper method of enjoying Chinese cuisine. One standardized menu suggested, "instead of individual orders, if a party of four orders a variety of single dishes to be served to all on individual plates after being brought to the table, a really portentious (*sic*) spread may be secured at a trifling expense. Try it."

Migration was slow to alter food habits in China. Because the sending regions were limited, culinary adaptations from South-east Asia or the Americas did not spread widely in the countryside. Remittances from migrant workers did allow many families to eat better than they would have otherwise, but they usually sought to join the local gentry and followed their eating habits. Western foods first appeared in colonial hotels, and even residents of Hong Kong only began to sample them in the 1940s in specialized tea cafés.

## Spaghetti and meatballs

Regional cuisines varied widely in Italy, and the macaroni common in the south differed greatly from the polenta and risotto eaten in the north. Unlike the Chinese, whose migrants came almost exclusively from a few coastal regions, Italians from throughout the peninsula left home and spread their diverse cooking traditions around the world. In the early modern era, skilled artisans, generally from the north, introduced Renaissance civilization throughout Europe. Migrants from Piedmont and Lombardy continued to follow well-trodden paths to Switzerland and France in the nineteenth century, while also setting off for new destinations in South America, particularly the cities of Buenos Aires and São Paulo. The Bourbon Kingdom of the Two Sicilies had long contributed migrants to the Spanish Empire, but after unification, southern peasants also departed in great numbers to the United States. More than 14,000,000 migrants left Italy from 1876 to 1914, and half eventually returned home.

Italians generally avoided the indentures common to Asian workers, but they nevertheless often served in labor gangs to pay off debts to *padroni* (patrons), who arranged their travel and at times their food as well. Male workers usually ended up in construction, mining, and commercial agriculture, while a minority of female migrants, who arrived in greater numbers than Chinese women, went into the textile and garment industries. In North America, migrants were segregated into ethnic communities, called "Little Italies," that quickly gained criminal stereotypes. To prejudiced eyes, Italians were potential mafiosi, just as Chinese were feared as opium addicts. But although outsiders reduced the ethnic community to a homogenized "dago," Italian Americans recognized distinct regional dialects and thereby maintained connections to their places of origin. According to a 1930s' survey: "Every district, city and province of Italy is represented in New York by its restaurant, which serves as a meeting place for fellow townsmen."

Restaurateurs and home cooks went to great expense to reproduce local recipes, and the agricultural abundance of the Americas made it possible for common workers to eat like the rich back home. Italian festival foods including eel, anchovies, and dried codfish – bizarre items to mainstream consumers – were imported by ethnic grocers along with large quantities of cheese, olive oil, and dried mushrooms. Italian butchers meanwhile specialized in lamb, goat, organ meats, and particular sausages eaten at Christmas or Easter. A resident of Boston's North End explained: "Italians do not go to the nearest store for groceries but went to the store they knew carried their favorite regional foods." Americans ate relatively few salads in the nineteenth century, so migrants raised their own tomatoes, greens, and figs in small kitchen gardens, even in crowded New York tenements. They also produced homemade versions of Chianti wine, affectionately dubbed "dago red" as a reversal of ethnic slurs. In the process of provisioning themselves, Italians introduced mainstream consumers to broccoli, fennel, celery, and other vegetables, at the same time providing invaluable expertise to the California wine industry.

Italian migrants made many of the same contributions in South as in North America, but their efforts tended to receive greater recognition. Most ended up in manual labor either in the meatpacking plants of Buenos Aires or the coffee plantations of São Paulo. The few who arrived with capital prospered and became stalwarts of the local bourgeoisie. Yet even common workers were welcomed into the national life rather than being segregated into ethnic enclaves. Milanese veal cutlets and meat tortes, rare festival foods in Italy, became common Brazilian dishes, as did salads and polenta. Argentine cookbook author Doña Petrona Carrizo de Gandulfo included risottos and fresh pasta dishes in her bestselling volume. Along with German migrants, Italians also contributed to the local wine industry. Latin Americans thus preferred northern Italian dishes, unlike the United States, where Neapolitan and Sicilian macaroni were more common.

Moreover, although Latin Americans embraced migrant foods, North Americans clung much longer to Anglo culinary traditions. As migrations peaked in the first decade of the twentieth century, educators sought to indoctrinate the new arrivals into the local culture, including pot roast and baked beans. One social worker reported a visit to an Italian home with the words: "Still eating spaghetti, not yet assimilated." Yet the migrants developed different notions of community and nation. An Italian American later recalled:

It never occurred to me that just being a citizen of the United States meant that I was an "American." "Americans" were people who ate peanut butter and jelly on mushy white bread that came out of a plastic package.

Italian food gradually began to attract the interest of North Americans, starting with Bohemian artists and writers, and restaurateurs later lured customers with promises of cheap tourism – singing waiters and checkered tablecloths – and cheap food. The food industry further transformed Italian dishes, particularly the canned pasta of Italian chef Hector Boiardi, who spelled his name Boyardee for easier pronunciation. Italian Americans eventually filled an entire menu with spaghetti and meatballs, pepperoni pizza, and other dishes that bore scant resemblance to the foods of the homeland. Indeed, the ethnic Italian community invented a common national cuisine that has never actually existed in Italy.

Nevertheless, sojourners, called *golondrini* (swallows) because of their regular migrations back and forth across the Atlantic, left an imprint on working-class Italian food habits. Money saved while working abroad allowed them to maintain the more affluent diets they had become accustomed to in the Americas. Less-fortunate neighbors criticized the *americani* for their extravagant consumption habits, eating "meat and fancy dishes" rather than subsistence peasant foods. But as a result, festive dishes, macaroni and tomatoes, plentiful cheese, espresso with sugar, and other former luxuries became everyday foods for workers and peasants as well as for the urban bourgeoisie.

## Conclusion

The experience of nineteenth-century proletarian migration had a number of common denominators. Italians and Chinese were invaluable to the economic development of the Americas, working on the railroads, in farming, and construction, yet in the popular mind they were associated with criminality, the mafia and opium dens. Migrants from Europe and Asia generally consumed a far richer diet, particularly more meat, yet their foods were at the same time impoverished by the lack of familiar vegetables. These creolized cuisines appealed first to Bohemians and members of the working classes, but eventually gained wide acceptance in the new societies, even when the natives continued to fear the foreigners racially.

Differences between Chinese and Italians derived largely from such prejudices. Although Italians were not always considered white, Chinese were always racial outsiders. Such discrimination hindered the transition of migrants from bachelor societies to established families, while anti-miscegenation laws prevented intermarriage with Anglos. Nevertheless, widespread return migration occurred not simply because of discrimination and the inability to find marriage partners, but also from attachments to family and homes. Another difference arose from the lack of support given to Chinese migrants by the Qing dynasty compared with the Italian state after unification in 1870, which saw the Italians overseas as a form of imperial colonization. Yet despite the state-building efforts of elites, migrants often saw little incompatibility between being simultaneously Chinese-Peruvian or Italian-Canadian. Such attitudes also influenced the blending of food habits, which created distinctive creole cuisines, drawing from both their birthplace and their adopted homes. Patterns of culinary exchange, established by Chinese and Italians travelers in the nineteenth century, also helped twentieth-century migrants to create a global palate.

## Further reading

The best general survey of migration is Dirk Hoerder, *Cultures in Contact: World Migration in the Second Millennium* (Durham, NC: Duke University Press, 2002). For Italians, see Donna R. Gabaccia, *Italy's Many Diasporas* (London: UCL Press, 2000); Donna R. Gabaccia, *We Are What We Eat: Ethnic Food and the Making of Americans* (Cambridge, MA: Harvard University Press, 1998); and Hasia Diner, *Hungering for America: Italian, Irish, and Jewish Foodways in the Age of Migration* (Cambridge, MA: Harvard University Press, 2001). On the Chinese, Yong Chen, *Chinese San Francisco, 1850–1943: A Trans-Pacific Community* (Stanford, CA: Stanford University Press, 2000); Sucheng Chan, *This Bittersweet Soil: The Chinese in California Agriculture, 1860–1910* (Berkeley, CA: University of California Press, 1986); Adam McKeown, *Chinese Migrant Networks and Cultural Change: Peru, Chicago, Hawaii, 1900–1936* (Chicago: University of Chicago Press, 2001); J. A. G. Roberts, *From China to Chinatown: Chinese Food in the West* (London: Reaktion Books, 2002); and David Y. H. Wu and Tan Chee-beng (eds), *Changing Chinese Foodways in Asia* (Hong Kong: Chinese University Press, 2001).

# Part III

# The global palate

Cuisines were already thoroughly globalized at the dawn of the twentieth century. Early modern crop diffusions had introduced the most productive grains and livestock to virtually all regions where they could be raised efficiently. Chile peppers, citrus fruits, and other new condiments and spices had meanwhile reshaped taste preferences around the world. Nineteenth-century industrialization contributed further to the integration of global provisioning. Improved transportation and colonial conquests made it possible for meat from the Australian outback and South American pampas, as well as coffee and tea from tropical plantations in Bengal and Burundi, to become everyday commodities on European tables. Proletarian migrations added even greater variety to the international mix of food habits in urban areas from London to Lima, where residents and visitors could sample the cuisines of five continents within a few city blocks. The emergence of a "global palate" in the twentieth century thus represented not a radical departure from the past but rather the intensification of existing cross-cultural connections.

Nor did the twentieth century bring steady progress toward global abundance; war and dictatorship revived the specter of famine for affluent citizens of Western Europe. Industrial warfare in an age of nationalism made hunger a tool of military planners. During the two world wars, rival powers carried out blockades and strategic bombing to reduce the enemy population to submission. The Great Depression of the 1930s further undermined the economic privilege of industrial societies. To survive such desperate circum-stances, dictatorships and liberal democracies alike asserted ever greater control over food supplies.

The resulting nationalization of food politics shifted the balance of power within the public sphere. Governments sought to harness the wealth of agri-cultural productivity to achieve industrial modernization, but these campaigns intensified existing struggles between the countryside and the city. On an even more extreme scale, fascist dictators believed they had to transform popular diets in order to achieve national greatness and avoid dependence on imported foods. The Cold War opened a new front in the struggle for economic and political supremacy. Although the threat of nuclear confrontation and proxy wars dominated strategic considerations, in Europe the rivalry between capitalism and communism was fought out primarily through propaganda. Marxist dialectical materialism promised workers a paradise on earth, and the failure to provide consumer goods or even adequately feed their citizens ultimately undermined communist regimes. Moreover, the politics of food offered new opportunities for women to gain influence outside the home. While housewives had participated in food riots of the past, in the twentieth century their efforts to feed and care for their families provided an important justification for women's suffrage. Maternal discourses thus offered a springboard to broader political roles.

Perhaps the greatest political change in the second half of the twentieth century was the downfall of European empires. The devastation of two world wars left the colonial powers unable to prevent the spread of independence movements through Africa and Asia from the 1940s to 1970s. The leaders of these movements dreamed of transforming their traditional societies into modern industrial nations, yet significant obstacles lay in their path. Attempts to forge unified nations foundered on ethnic hostilities left over from colonial boundaries, which were based on European rivalries rather than social realities. Moreover, imperial trade and investment had been designed to extract wealth for the metropolis rather than assure balanced development within the colonies. Nevertheless, in attempting to create urban, industrial economies, the new elites often repeated the mistakes of their colonial tutors. Agricultural modernization programs emphasized European cash crops rather than more viable local alternatives, and the profits were siphoned away from small farmers to pay for grandiose, often ill-conceived industrial projects.

By the end of the twentieth century, many had begun to question the viability of agribusiness in Europe and North America. Even though heavily subsidized, small farms had become increasingly incapable of attaining economic viability. Moreover, agricultural productivity had been achieved through heavy inputs of chemical fertilizers and pesticides, while meat supplies depended on feedlots and antibiotics. New technologies such as genetically modified (GM) foods raised even more intense concerns about the long-term effects on human and environmental health, worries that were magnified by the companies' refusal to test their products adequately. The pace of change was equally rapid for consumers, who came to depend on fast food chains and packaged convenience foods, despite the consequences in poor nutrition and obesity from such choices. Particularly among the young, balanced meals eaten in a domestic setting became increasingly rare in modern societies.

Paradoxically, however, these changes coincided with a growing interest in culinary experimentation. Continued high levels of global migration led to constantly changing opportunities for ethnic dining, as the lower-class Chinese and Italian restaurants of the nineteenth century went upscale with regional cuisines, to be replaced in the United States by Mexican and Vietnamese newcomers. Food also served as an important focus of tourism, which was an increasingly vital sector of the international economy. Finally, as advertising and consumer culture took on international dimensions, brands such as McDonald's and Coca-Cola became common in even the most remote villages. The global palate had become truly ubiquitous.

# Chapter 10

# Guns and butter

At the beginning of the twentieth century, industrial workers in Western Europe had finally gained access to a diet of previously unknown luxury – daily meat, white bread, and fresh vegetables – only to see it vanish again in the misery of global war and depression. The twin currents of industrialization and nationalism conspired to mobilize entire continents for warfare from 1914–18 and again from 1937–45. In an age of total war, hunger became simply another weapon to reduce the enemy's will to fight. World War I also fueled the rise of totalitarian states that were ruthlessly determined to control food supplies in order to ensure national survival. Between war and dictatorship, Europe reverted to a pre-modern moral economy in which life depended on uncertain entitlement to limited supplies of food.

The politics of food had nevertheless changed with the rise of nations. Tensions had always existed between food producers in the countryside and consumers in the cities, but modern states upset this balance through attempts to finance industrialization by extracting wealth from agriculture and by shifting rural labor to urban factories. Authoritarian governments in particular sought to nationalize diets, and their efforts to organize food supplies took advantage of the supposed threat of potential enemies, whether foreign producers or "unpatriotic" merchants who profited from troubled times. The growing weight of urban society also led to a new form of consumer politics as formerly marginalized groups including workers and women asserted demands of citizenship based on entitlement to the basic necessities of life. From the late 1940s to the late 1980s, the Cold War between capitalism and communism turned largely on the question of which system could best provide such material benefits for the common people.

## Wars of attrition

Europeans cheered the call to arms in August 1914, but their martial enthusiasm soon drowned in the bloody stalemate of trench warfare. As successive waves of soldiers fell to machine guns on the Front, another war of attrition was fought at sea; the Allies blockaded the German surface fleet in port, while U-boats hunted commercial shipping on the Atlantic. All the European powers proved vulnerable to economic warfare, even such traditional food exporters as France and Russia, where provisioning networks broke down under the strains of mobilization. In Britain, which imported two-thirds of its foodstuffs on the eve of war, Prime Minister David Lloyd George later declared: "We came nearer to defeat owing to food shortage than we did from anything else." The French, recalling that hunger had fueled the revolutions of 1789 and 1848, likewise struggled to import more grain and thereby avoid the need for rationing. Indeed, the intense famines suffered by the Germans undermined support for the war effort and created revolutionary conditions in Berlin. The inability of the Russian government to feed its people precipitated the collapse of the tsarist regime and ushered in the communist revolution.

At the outbreak of war, the British Navy closed off the North Sea to Germany, which imported not only a third of its foodstuffs but also the chemical fertilizers needed for domestic agriculture. Germans had long been familiar with ersatz foods, for example, drinking chicory in place of coffee, and the blockade took effect only gradually, as consumers fell back on *Kriegsbrot* and *Kriegsbier* (war bread and war beer) made of various substitutes. By the fall of 1915, rationing had inspired butter riots in the capital along with wider consumer protests against profiteering. After the devastating failure of the potato harvest in 1916, the population subsisted on nothing but turnips. Hunger stalled the war effort; when German soldiers broke through the enemy lines, they stopped to search for food. The home front was equally desperate, as a Danish visitor, Asta Neilson, discovered when an emaciated horse collapsed in the streets of Berlin.

> In an instant, as though they had been lying in ambush, women armed with kitchen knives stormed out of the apartment buildings and fell upon the cadaver. They screamed and hit one another to get the best pieces, as the steaming blood sprayed their faces.

Malnutrition killed as many as 700,000 civilians, on top of Germany's 1,800,000 battlefield casualties. The injustice of black marketeering also deprived the Kaiser of legitimacy, leading food protesters to join striking workers in a revolutionary movement that shook Berlin in November 1918.

Meanwhile in Russia, a similar failure by the tsarist government to supply food to hungry workers allowed the communists to seize power. Russia had entered the war as a major exporter of grain, but commercial networks running south by river barge to Crimean ports were ill-equipped to supply soldiers on the Western Front. The Ministry of Agriculture imposed strict controls on exchange, hoping to eliminate middlemen, but succeeded only in disrupting markets throughout the country. In the black-earth regions of southern Russia, peasants resisted government requisitions of surplus grain, while those farming less productive land in the north, along with urban workers, found it difficult to obtain basic subsistence. By the end of 1916 – Germany's "turnip winter" – government authority had broken down, leaving the food supply and the entire war effort in chaos. The failure of grain shipments to reach Petrograd in February 1917 delivered the final blow. Local officials were unprepared even for rationing, and the ineffectual tsar abdicated in the face of striking workers and army mutineers. The provisional government proved no more capable of distributing food, and in October it fell to a small but determined cadre of Bolsheviks under V. I. Lenin.

Once in power, Lenin faced the dilemma of creating an effective food supply system in a time of civil war. Shortages worsened in the spring of 1918 after the Treaty of Brest-Litovsk ceded control of the rich Ukrainian farmland to Germany. To make up for these losses, the Bolsheviks increased grain requisitions in other regions, particularly Siberia, provoking peasant rebellions beneficial to the White Army, which fought to restore the tsar. Over the next three years, the Red Army gradually re-conquered the separatist provinces to form the Soviet Union. Notwithstanding the fierce ideological divisions between Red and White leaders, peasant soldiers often saw the conflict in terms of bread, as Stepan Ivanovich Portugeis observed: "This 'war' was no more than a punitive food-supply expedition on the part of the hungry and a food-supply boycott on the part of those with food."

Food assumed equal prominence in the rhetoric of anti-war protesters and suffragists. Jane Addams, a leader of the Settlement House movement in Chicago, which sought to improve the livelihood of poor immigrants, observed that "peace and bread had become inseparably connected." The international Women's Peace Party argued for suffrage on the basis that the maternal qualities of women were needed to offset the aggressive nature of men in politics. In the war's aftermath, women won the vote in Britain, Canada, and the United States.

## Food for the state

The struggle for victory in World War I brought unprecedented state intervention in the economies of Europe and North America, and food policy remained crucial for governments in the post-war era. Soviet leaders continued to tighten their grip on the countryside in order to consolidate the communist revolution and to support their program of rapid industrialization. Fascist dictatorships that arose in Italy and Germany during the 1920s and 1930s likewise considered agriculture vital to their quest for national greatness. Even liberal democratic governments took an active role in food provisioning to counter the Great Depression.

Benito Mussolini's fascist regime in Italy directed state control of food toward the ideal of "alimentary sovereignty" – self-sufficiency in provisioning. This policy fit with the broader goal of nationalizing the masses, previously divided by regional loyalties and class disparities, and reasserting Italian greatness. In 1925, three years after seizing power, Mussolini declared a Battle for Grain in order to free Italy from the "slavery" of imported agriculture. Yet this campaign came at the expense of profitable export crops, including fresh produce, citrus fruits, and olives, while also decreasing the diversity of the Italian diet. Declining standards of living did not deter the dictator, who callously observed: "Fortunately the Italian population has not yet accustomed itself to eat many times a day, and possessing a modest level of living, it feels deficiency and suffering less."

Mussolini's alliance with Adolf Hitler compounded the shortages by diverting Italian resources to the Nazi war machine. The invasion of Ethiopia in 1935 had strained domestic supplies, both because of international embargoes protesting fascist aggression and because the occupied territory never achieved self-sufficiency. With the outbreak of World War II, Mussolini exchanged Italian farm products and migrant workers for German war material in the hopes of contributing to Axis conquests, although Hitler did not share this vision of partnership. Eventually the black market became the only available source of food. As Mussolini's regime collapsed in 1944, the mayor of Monza lamented the flight of former fascist supporters to Italian versions of capitalism or socialism: "Collectivist principles are magnificent ideals – bread for our brains – but the stomach does not have ideals: either it is conservative – if it is full – or it is anarchist – if it is empty."

Meanwhile, Joseph Stalin's program of agricultural collectivization in the Soviet Union went even further in asserting state control over food supplies. Ever since Karl Marx had denounced "the idiocy of rural life," communist leaders had regarded agricultural workers as unreliable allies in class warfare. The New Economic Policy of the mid-1920s represented a truce after the grain struggles of the Civil War, but during this interlude, peasants retained the bulk of their own production, in part because state-run factories offered little for rural consumption. By the end of the decade, Stalin had eliminated rivals within the Communist Party, and when peasants resisted new grain requisitions, he decreed the creation of collective farms and the "liquidation of the kulaks as a class." In practice, kulaks were not a class of wealthy peasants but rather a label for potential opposition leaders. A Soviet activist described one such victim: "He has a sick wife, five children and not a crumb of bread in the house. And that's what we call a kulak!" Urban communists simply misunderstood the countryside, interpreting peasant factiousness as class conflict. When confronted with the expropriation of livestock and farming equipment, villages united against collectivization. As with eighteenth-century food riots, women often led these rebellions against Soviet authority, and resistance was particularly strong in the peripheral regions of the Ukraine, Kazakhstan, and Siberia.

The industrial program of the First Five Year Plan (1929–1934) received the highest priority from Soviet leaders, leaving collectivization to be carried out in a haphazard fashion. Stalin's fascination with enormous factories encouraged a mistaken belief that farming likewise had endless potential for economies of scale. Tractors, in particular, held out the promise of industrial agriculture, and even before they could be produced, the government organized giant farms more appropriate to the new machines than to the plows they actually had. Such failures of planning point to the inexperience of administrators, who were generally urban workers rather than politically suspect peasants. Dekulakization had already eliminated the most productive farmers, and those who remained offered passive resistance. Rather than allow the expropriation of livestock, many peasants slaughtered their own animals, celebrating one last feast before entering the collective. When questioned why they done so, they replied with feigned naïveté: "There will be no need for draft animals on the kolkhoz – we will have tractors."

The mistakes of Soviet agrarian policy culminated in the tragic Ukrainian famine. Central planners invariably set lofty goals – the better to inspire heroic efforts from the proletariat – but while unrealistic industrial targets had few consequences for factory workers, setting grain quotas too high meant starvation in the countryside. Peasants could feed themselves only by stealing from the collective, which the Soviet authorities condemned as capitalist sabotage. For their part, peasants perceived such repression as a breakdown of the traditional social contract, whereby rulers offered protection during times of hunger in return for work. Thus, the mutual incomprehension widened. During the terrible winter of 1932–33, as starvation spread among the peasantry, party cadres redoubled their efforts to impound food and satisfy production quotas. One woman defiantly shouted: "Take it. Take everything away. There's still a pot of borscht on the stove. It's plain, got no meat. But still it's got beets, taters 'n' cabbage. And it's salted! Better take it, comrade citizens!" Many millions died of hunger that year, with the worst losses centered in the most productive agricultural regions, especially the Ukraine. Soviet policies proved self-defeating in the long run as large numbers of farmers gave up working on the collectives.

Western democracies sought a middle path between the extremes of fascism and communism, but the Great Depression prompted massive economic intervention to prevent the collapse of capitalism. In the United States, business failures and bank closings drove nearly a third of the labor force out of work. Yet even as bread lines formed in the cities, low food prices threatened farmers with bankruptcy. President Franklin Delano Roosevelt, elected in 1932, stimulated economic recovery through the Works Progress Administration (WPA) and other New Deal programs. For farmers, the Agricultural Adjustment Act set price supports and offered payments not to cultivate surplus crops. Nevertheless, benefits were calculated according to production rather than need, so the wealthiest farmers received the most assistance. Smallholders, tenants, and sharecroppers, ineligible for support, were driven off the land. "I bought tractors on the money the government give me and got shet o' my renters," an Oklahoma landlord explained. "They got their choice – California or WPA."

Once in California, migrants worked on large commercial farms. Agribusiness prospered with New Deal largesse, particularly Bureau of Reclamation water projects. Farmers in the San Joaquin and Sacramento River valleys had largely depleted groundwater reserves by the 1920s, but the Central Valley Project, begun in 1935, established a network of dams to capture drainage from the Sierra Nevada Mountains. Although intended by law to benefit small farms, irrigation instead subsidized entrenched corporate interests. "Arkie" and "Okie" refugees, having been displaced from their homes by tractors and drought, ended up living in primitive shanties and harvesting cotton, fruit, and vegetables. The former occupants of these labor camps, Hispanic and Asian migrant workers, had largely been repatriated as a result of the Depression. In the United States, as in Europe, state-supported agricultural mechanization had driven independent smallholders from the land to make room for corporate farms – thus providing a capitalist version of collectivization.

Rival claims to national power collided again in World War II, and as before, supplies of food and material shaped military planning. Thus, although racism inspired the broad outlines of Hitler's expansionist policies, the Nazi blitzkrieg against Russia in 1941 targeted in particular Ukrainian agriculture and the Caucasus oilfields. Japan's Pacific campaign of 1941, including the bombing of Pearl Harbor, likewise aimed to secure access to South-east Asian raw materials. Warfare continued to escalate against non-combatants through blockades, submarine warfare, and most notoriously, strategic bombing. Civilian contributions in agricultural and industrial labor and food rationing thus assumed true heroism. The Allies' control of the material wealth of the Americas, Africa, and much of Asia helped ensure their ultimate victory.

## The kitchen debate

With the defeat of fascism, the United States and the Soviet Union poised for battle over the ruins of Europe. The Red Army imposed satellite governments throughout Eastern Europe, and many feared that hunger would help socialist parties win elections in the West as well. To counter this threat, in 1947, the Marshall Plan offered assistance to European economic reconstruction. The nuclear-armed rival alliances, NATO and the Warsaw Pact, never came to blows, notwithstanding such confrontations as the Berlin blockade of 1948, when airlifted food and coal allowed the western outpost to survive a Soviet embargo. Instead, the Cold War in Europe was fought largely through propaganda, as capitalist leaders trumpeted the superiority of free enterprise in providing material benefits for consumers, while critics questioned the justice of a system that maintained segregated lunch counters in the United States.

Coca-Cola's global advertising spearheaded the capitalist propaganda campaign, although even Western allies questioned such unrestrained consumerism. The soft drink company had only modest European sales before World War II, so the U.S. government financed bottling plants behind the battlefront to boost troop morale. Coke followed up this advantage with massive publicity in the post-war era, to the dismay of European brewers, vintners, and mineral water producers. Opposition was particularly strong in France, where critics denounced the soft drink as unhealthy, addictive, and a threat to the national culture. Nevertheless, under State Department pressure, the government refrained from issuing a ban, and Coke became popular throughout Western Europe.

One of the most dramatic moments in the propaganda struggle occurred in the so-called "kitchen debate," of July 24, 1959, between Premier Nikita Khrushchev and Vice-President Richard Nixon. The exchange took place at the American National Exhibition in Moscow, as the two leaders toured a model home equipped with televisions, kitchen appliances, and other consumer goods. "Anything that makes women work less is good," declared Nixon, pointing out the latest model dishwasher. "We don't think of women in terms of capitalism," Khrushchev replied. "We think better of them." The Soviet premier also condemned the inefficiency of producing so many different kinds of gadgets. "Don't you have a machine that puts food into the mouth and pushes it down?"

Yet throughout the kitchen debate, Khrushchev remained defensive because the Soviet Union could not match the capitalist world in supplying consumer goods. Disparities grew even wider in subsequent decades, and during the Détente years of the 1970s, the Soviet Union came to rely on massive grain purchases from the United States to feed its people. The strategic dangers of this policy were driven home when President Jimmy Carter terminated the sales in response to the Soviet invasion of Afghanistan in 1979. Communist governments in Eastern Europe likewise felt the pressure from food shortages. In 1980, the doubling of meat prices in Poland sparked nationwide protests that helped establish the Solidarity Union of shipyard workers, whose demands for political freedom sent shock waves through the Communist Bloc. The limited reforms of Premier Mikhail Gorbachev's perestroika, adopted in the mid-1980s, merely whetted appetites for more consumer goods, thereby hastening the fall of the Soviet Union.

One final glimpse behind the scenes of the kitchen debate offers a revealing perspective on the Cold War. The chairman of Pepsi Cola accompanied Nixon to Moscow and negotiated an exclusive marketing agreement with Soviet authorities, albeit using state-run bottling plants. As a result, Pepsi became identified with the inefficiency of communism, while Coke symbolized the forbidden pleasures of Western consumerism. When the Berlin Wall fell in 1989, Coke swept through Eastern European markets, nullifying Pepsi's initial advantage. Even Khrushchev's quip about an eating machine was taken straight from Hollywood – Charlie Chaplin's cinematic critique of industrial capitalism, *Modern Times* (1936). The dialectical materialism of Marxism held out the promise of consumer goods that Soviet leaders ultimately found impossible to supply, thus dooming the experiment with communism.

## Conclusion

Twentieth-century attempts to organize society by both fascist and socialist states reached the most basic level, their citizens' daily bread. Food policies served as tools for both political centralization and economic modernization. Yet in totalitarian regimes, as in liberal democracies, consumer demands retained potent political force. Rulers might blame shortages on supposed enemies of the people, whether kulak peasants or foreign profiteers, but citizens ultimately held their governments responsible for assuring their material well-being.

Important changes can be seen in comparing the politics of food over time. Whereas the food riots of the eighteenth century were often conservative attempts to buttress a moral economy based on paternalistic values, those of the twentieth century could be far more progressive. During World War I, for example, working-class women in Berlin began to assert rights of citizenship based on the entitlement to food. The Solidarity Union in Poland likewise tapped deeply felt sentiments through the demand for meat, and then channeled that visceral response into a broader political program that ultimately helped free the Communist Bloc. Political movements that start with women in the kitchen can therefore reverberate through the halls of government.

The terrible regression in European living standards over the first half of the twentieth century prompted the recognition of food as a basic human right. In 1941, President Roosevelt declared freedom from want to be one of the foundations of a moral society. Adequate food was likewise enshrined in the Universal Declaration of Human Rights of the United Nations. In the post-war era, Europe regained its former prosperity, but former colonies found even basic health and nutrition difficult to achieve amid Cold War and population growth.

## Further reading

On World War I, C. Paul Vincent, *The Politics of Hunger: The Allied Blockade of Germany, 1915–1919* (Athens, OH: Ohio University Press, 1985); Belinda J. Davis, *Home Fires Burning: Food, Politics, and Everyday Life in World War I Berlin* (Chapel Hill, NC: University of North Carolina Press, 2000); and Lars T. Lih, *Bread and Authority in Russia, 1914–1921* (Berkeley, CA: University of California Press, 1990). On the inter-war years, Carol Helstosky, *Garlic and Oil: Politics and Food in Italy* (London: Berg, 2004); Robert Conquest, *The Harvest of Sorrow: Soviet Collectivization and the Terror-Famine* (New York: Oxford University Press, 1986); Sheila Fitzpatrick, *Stalin's Peasants: Resistance and Survival in the Russian Village after Collectivization* (New York: Oxford University Press, 1994); James N. Gregory, *American Exodus: The Dust Bowl*

*Migration and Okie Culture in California* (New York: Oxford University Press, 1989); and Devra Weber, *Dark Sweat, White Gold: California Farm Workers, Cotton, and the New Deal* (Berkeley, CA: University of California Press, 1994). For the Cold War, Diane B. Kunz, *Butter and Guns: America's Cold War Economic Diplomacy* (New York: The Free Press, 1997); Richard Pells, *Not Like Us: How Europeans Have Loved, Hated, and Transformed American Culture since World War II* (New York: Basic Books, 1997).

# Chapter 11

# The Green Revolution

In the 1970s, as Western Europeans and North Americans grew complacent on the bounty of modern agriculture, their televisions began showing disturbing images of famine from Bangladesh, Ethiopia, and across the African Sahel. Children with bellies distended from hunger cried out for help, but relief workers faced difficult questions as they sought to deliver emergency supplies to devastated regions. Would food aid actually reach starving people or would warlords, often embroiled in Cold War conflicts, divert shipments to buy guns? If grain did arrive, would it undermine local agricultural markets and make it more difficult for the poor to feed themselves in the long term? Was immediate relief simply delaying an inevitable reckoning between population growth and environmental degradation, which would revive the Malthusian specter of general starvation? Pessimism abounded as many experts concluded that the planet simply could not support a projected population of over ten billion people by the end of the twenty-first century.

Yet others refused to share this gloom and argued that developing countries could support their growing numbers with modern technology. The application of high-yielding seed, irrigation, fertilizer, pesticides, and farm machinery brought about a veritable "Green Revolution" of agricultural productivity in countries such as Mexico, India, Turkey, and the Philippines. Output of the principal staples, maize, wheat, and rice, increased dramatically so that the number of undernourished people remained relatively stable – at slightly under a billion – although the world population more than doubled to six billion in the second half of the twentieth century. Optimists predicted that further advances in biotechnology, particularly the development of GM plants and animals, would ultimately ensure plentiful food for all. Critics countered that the Green Revolution provided not a cornucopia but rather a source of growing inequality as wealthy landholders employed technology to monopolize scarce land and water resources, further impoverishing the poorest farmers.

Debates over world hunger faced additional complications. Malthusian calculations of aggregate population numbers and food production levels obscured local inequalities in distribution that left many people starving even during plentiful harvests. Food shortages also took diverse forms, with some poor countries troubled by endemic undernourishment while others were more vulnerable to sudden famines. The demographic transition posed yet another dilemma for planners; families tended to have more children in the countryside than in cities, but it remained unclear whether declining fertility would offset the losses in agricultural production as farmland disappeared beneath urban sprawl.

The politics of forging unified nations from ethnically diverse colonies further hampered food policies. Independence leaders of the 1950s and 1960s sought to remedy the inequalities left by imperialism, but they often retained European biases as a result of metropolitan educations. Thus, they viewed great cities, modern industry, and even Western diets as hallmarks of development. Even without corrupt politicians, small farmers paid a disproportionate share of the burden for financing industrialization, as they had previously in Europe and North America. Land and other resources were taken away from subsistence agriculture to grow export commodities. The political threat of hungry masses also prompted heavy subsidies on urban food supplies, encouraging even greater migration to cities. Meanwhile, the slight nutritional advantage of imported grains over native staples did not offset the costs of depending on foreign supplies and further undermining local agriculture.

Nor could politicians in wealthy nations ignore the potential revolutionary violence of a hungry world. Agricultural modernization and population control were seen as essential complements to military alliances in containing communism. Not coincidentally, the principal beneficiaries of the Green Revolution were all nations considered vital for Cold War strategy. The World Bank and the International Monetary Fund likewise tailored development assistance to ensure economic stability in the interests of the western powers.

## Modernizing agriculture

The productivity gains of the Green Revolution resulted from a complex package of improved seeds, fertilizer, pesticides, and irrigation, but in addition to technological inputs, profound social transformations were needed to ameliorate poverty and hunger. Mexico and India, two champions of agricultural modernization, had each undergone such movements, the former with the agrarian revolution of Emiliano Zapata beginning in 1910 and the latter with Mahatma Gandhi's non-violent independence campaign, culminating in 1947. Yet in each case, reformers proved more successful in creating a dynamic agribusiness sector than in achieving social justice.

Although the traditional narrative of the Green Revolution focuses on a lineage of scientists running from experiment-minded gentlemen farmers of the eighteenth century to the Nobel Laureate plant pathologist Norman Borlaug, credit for agricultural innovation actually extends much further. The anonymous but observant peasant cultivators who incorporated forage grasses into crop rotations were crucial for increasing livestock and grain production in early modern Europe. Nor were such improvements limited to the West; Japanese farmers bred dwarf wheat and rice strains to intensify output. The nineteenth-century formalization of agricultural and veterinary science was likewise an international undertaking, with practitioners in Mexico as in the United States, and was conducted on experiment stations in both colonial India and the British metropolis.

The development of hybrid seeds, combining the best traits of different maize or wheat varieties, offered tremendous opportunities for increasing harvests. The first such hybrid seeds were sold commercially in the United States in the 1930s, and when Mexico joined the Allied Powers in World War II, the Rockefeller Foundation sent a survey team to improve the local agriculture. They discovered that seeds accommodated to the United States fared poorly in Mexican soil and therefore sought to recreate selective breeding programs with native samples at the national agricultural school in Chapingo. By the end of the 1940s, scientists had developed high yielding strains of Mexican maize as well as wheat varieties resistant to stem rust epidemics.

Additional inputs multiplied the gains from hybrid seeds. Damming rivers, particularly in the north-west, provided farmers with ample irrigation as well as hydroelectric power. Chemical fertilizers and pesticides likewise boosted productivity; indeed, strains of wheat grew so heavy that they actually keeled over before the harvest. Researchers solved the problem by crossing Mexican varieties with Japanese dwarf wheat so that the plants grew thick instead of tall. By the 1960s, Mexican maize harvests had tripled while wheat showed even greater improvements.

Yet aggregate production gains did not create general prosperity for Mexican farmers since few could afford the new technology. The revolutionary government had carried out extensive land reform, but peasants still lacked credit to purchase improved seed and other inputs. Hybrid maize required new seed each year, since leftovers from a previous harvest lost their higher yields when replanted. Government programs originally intended to benefit small farmers compounded the inequalities; extension agents focused their educational efforts on the largest landholders, who in turn received favorable treatment from purchasing agents of the government's urban food welfare program. Highly productive agribusiness depressed overall farm prices, forcing millions of peasants to abandon the land.

The uneven record of agricultural modernization was largely repeated in India. The greatest successes occurred in the north-western province of Punjab, where market-oriented peasants benefited from irrigation projects carried out at the end of the nineteenth century. Comprehensive land reform and consolidation after independence allowed small farmers to take full advantage of Green Revolution technology, starting in the 1960s. Local researchers bred their own improved wheat varieties, which became even more productive when crossed with Mexican strains. Farmers adopted a crop rotation of high yielding wheat followed by "miracle" rice strains developed at the Rockefeller-supported International Rice Research Institute in the Philippines, and originally based on peasant hybrids from Taiwan. Moreover, agricultural gains came to the Punjab without many of the social disruptions experienced by Mexico. Secure land tenure and few absentee landlords allowed small farmers to compete using family labor rather than mechanization.

Other regions of India reaped fewer benefits and greater unrest. In rice-growing regions such as West Bengal, hybrid seeds proved less adaptable to local microclimates. Maharashtra and other states lacking irrigation meanwhile suffered devastating droughts. Perhaps the greatest problem distributing the benefits of agricultural modernization, in India as in Mexico, was the widespread failure of land reform, since wealthy farmers took advantage of loopholes to accumulate large holdings, often with official connivance.

Ecologists also doubted the sustainability of Green Revolution productivity gains. Heavy irrigation depleted groundwater reserves, and intensive farming caused the build-up of salinity in the soil. Over time, insects acquired immunity to pesticides, even as the accumulation of toxic chemicals in the environment damaged the health of farm workers, consumers, and wildlife. The balance sheet of agricultural modernization thus remained unclear. Pessimists feared not only the inability to achieve future productivity gains but also the loss of much land currently in use. The question demanded even greater attention as population growth continued.

## Persistent famines

In contrast to the widely touted success of India and Mexico, many have dismissed Sub-Saharan Africa as a basket case, unable to grow enough food to keep pace with its exploding population. Although agricultural census data are notoriously inaccurate because of the tendency to ignore small peasant farms, food imports to the continent have risen steadily since the 1970s. Yet the image of a Malthusian race between production and population can be misleading without considering who has legal entitlement to food either by growing it themselves, by earning cash for market purchases, or through access to assistance programs. Most food imports have gone to relatively privileged urban dwellers, while starvation haunts the drought- and war-ravaged countryside. Danish economist Philip Raikes observed, "It is not countries which suffer hunger (and certainly not their political leaders), but specific disadvantaged sections of the population, often situated in particular hunger-prone areas."

India provides an instructive starting point for examining hunger in Africa. The Bengal Famine of 1943, which killed perhaps three million people, resulted primarily from wartime inflation. The failure of the previous harvest encouraged hoarding at a time when landless rural laborers could not afford to buy food. Famine Codes had existed since the 1880s, offering relief and public works, but in 1943 the colonial government simply did not invoke them. The avoidance of a similar famine after independence cannot be attributed to the Green Revolution, for population growth has actually outstripped agricultural gains and endemic undernourishment remains widespread. Nevertheless, despite a drought virtually every year somewhere in the subcontinent, India's democratically elected politicians have responded with relief efforts to avoid outright starvation. In 1972–73, for example, the government of Maharashtra carried out massive public works programs to prevent the unemployment that devastated wartime Bengal.

Short-sighted development programs and structural limitations have conspired against repeating Asian and Latin American agricultural improvements in Africa. Independence leaders throughout the continent established food purchasing boards, ostensibly to remedy the inequalities of colonialism, but their policies bred corruption and discriminated against small farmers. Colonial road networks designed for exporting raw materials likewise frustrated efficient internal markets. Moreover, Green Revolution technology often proved counterproductive in the thin, arid soils of Africa. High-yielding grains replaced the intercropping of drought-resistant native millet and sorghum, leaving farmers more vulnerable to bad weather. Water-intensive export crops, particularly cotton, quickly turned the ground saline, and irrigation projects spread malaria and river blindness. Perhaps most damaging were attempts to cultivate marginal lands traditionally used by pastoralists, first through forced settlement of nomadic societies and then by sending tractors onto the fragile soil. Sudan, which had avoided the worst of the Sahelian famines of 1965–73, suffered terribly in the mid-1980s as a result of such temporarily profitable but ultimately devastating agribusiness.

The Ethiopian famines of the 1970s and 1980s illustrate the deadly combination of drought, entitlement failure, and war. Local crop failures began among northern farmers in 1972, but when journalists finally mobilized foreign aid in late 1973, it arrived too late to help most victims. Relief efforts actually diverted supplies from where they were most needed by this point. Famine had spread to southern pastoralists, who sold their livestock into a glutted market, leaving them with insufficient money to purchase grain. Emperor Haile Selassie, having callously ignored the suffering, was overthrown in 1974, and a new socialist regime implemented land reform. Then an even worse drought struck in 1984–85, particularly in the north, where Western powers had sponsored an insurgency to prevent the spread of communism in Africa. Widespread media attention, including the Live Aid Concert organized by singer Bob Geldof, brought massive foreign assistance, but aid workers could not reach the most desperate victims in the war-torn north. Ultimately, the famine killed more than a million people.

Yet such disasters must be balanced against numerous examples of famines averted. Cape Verde suffered uninterrupted drought from 1968 to 1986, but intensive relief programs, first by the Portuguese colonial government, then after 1975 by a socialist one-party state, not only avoided catastrophe, but actually improved nutrition following independence. In Botswana, despite a booming diamond industry, rural incomes including mining remittances, declined steadily during the 1970s. Nevertheless, when drought struck in the early 1980s, the democratic government established an entitlement program to prevent famine. Comparing the success of Zimbabwe in the 1980s with the starvation two decades later after the dictatorial turn of President Robert Mugabe demonstrates that diverse policies and economic systems can avoid famine as long as governments remain open and pluralist.

Western aid has achieved mixed results in developing countries. Beginning in 1954, the United States exported large quantities of surplus grain under Public Law 480, known as Food for Peace. In addition to supporting domestic farm prices, the program was used explicitly for Cold War purposes. India received the bulk of sales in the first decade, followed by South Vietnam and Israel from the mid-1960s to the 1970s. After 1975, the program declined precipitously, along with U.S. surpluses, at just the time Africa most needed outside assistance. Nevertheless, the urban middle classes of Nigeria and other countries had acquired an expensive taste for foreign grains that could not be grown domestically. Unquestionably, Oxfam and other donors performed a vital function in times of need, but their actions often received disproportionate press coverage compared with local assistance programs.

In dealing with famines, general healthcare is as important as food entitlement, since hunger leaves people vulnerable to other diseases. Women and children are particularly at risk because local custom often deprives them of available food when developmentally they need it most. The AIDS epidemic poses new risks of famine by killing the most productive adults, leaving orphans and the elderly unable to provide for themselves. Now more than ever, Africa needs assistance from the outside and needs wise leadership at home.

## Mad cows and GM imperialism

The technology of modern agriculture has provoked increasing dissatisfaction in the developed world as well. Having forgotten the threat of hunger, consumers in North America and Western Europe have become concerned about the healthiness of foods and environmental sustainability, questions that have grown ever more complex as novel scientific discoveries transform the food chain.

The practice of crossing genes between different plants and animals prompted widespread debate at the turn of the millennium. Advocates of the new technology promise higher protein grains and reduced chemicals in the food chain as plants began containing their own pesticides. Opponents worry about the health effects of such plants as well as the ecological consequences of gene transfers in the wild. One of the most common GM crops, Bt maize, has been shown to adversely affect bees, ladybugs, and monarch butterflies.

The extension of private property rights over the common agricultural heritage also provoked outrage, for example, among the Zuni Pueblo of Arizona when a company trademarked a brand of "Zuni Corn." Demands for labeling GM and organic foods have begun to reverse the nineteenth-century commoditization of grains, as people become willing to pay more to know how their foods were produced.

Livestock-raising practices also elicited widespread concern. Chicken became a daily meat in the United States only with the development of industrial penning and processing plants in the 1960s, but such methods cause widespread salmonella contamination and avian flu epidemics, notwithstanding high levels of antibiotic usage. Over-fishing threatens maritime ecosystems, even as the search for cattle pasture contributes to tropical deforestation. Because of the inefficiency of meat production, which requires seven pounds of grain for each pound of beef, stockmen fed cattle the rendered remains of dead animals. This practice was widely banned in the mid-1990s after outbreaks of bovine spongiform encephalopathy (BSE), popularly known as "mad cow disease." The epidemic spread worldwide, and a human variant, Creutzfeldt-Jakob disease, has killed at least forty-three people in Britain.

Under such pressures, the food chain has become an increasing site of international conflict. A ban on British cattle exports during the BSE epidemic caused a crisis within the European Union until cases of the disease were discovered on the Continent as well. European consumers also led campaigns against GM technology, which U.S. officials dismissed as agricultural protectionism. Disputes between Europe and the United States over the global spread of GM crops meanwhile dragged developing countries into a new form of imperial rivalry. During a drought in 2002, for example, Zambia was forced to reject a shipment of U.S. food aid for fear that it would contaminate local crops and thus cut off future exports to the European Union. Continued globalization threatens to intensify such conflicts.

## Conclusion

The precarious balance between population growth and food production, emphasized by Thomas Malthus at the beginning of the nineteenth century, remains vital two hundred years later. While industrialization is heralded as the solution, the greatest famine of the twentieth century resulted from socialist China's Great Leap Forward development program. Yet the capitalist mantra of "getting prices right," shared by nineteenth-century liberals and contemporary international agencies, may be as unrealistic for Africa today as it was for Ireland during the potato famine if markets adjust only through massive starvation.

Agrarian reform and the Green Revolution have been most successful in facilitating the global spread of capitalist agriculture. Notwithstanding the justifiable fears of handing power to unelected corporate officials, a world of six billion people simply does not have the option of abandoning modern agriculture entirely and embracing a romanticized peasant past. However flawed the development programs of African, Asian, and Latin American countries may be, the alternative is to condemn their citizens to indefinite misery, thus making permanent the inequalities of colonialism. Without the hope of improved material conditions, impoverished peoples will provide a never-ending source of foot soldiers against Western modernity. Thus, the triumph of the Cold War in exalting the McDonald's hamburger as a universal ideal threatens to initiate a new era of global conflict.

## Further reading

On the origins of the Green Revolution, Joseph Cotter, *Troubled Harvest: Agronomy and Revolution in Mexico, 1880–2002* (New York: Praeger, 2003); and Himmat Singh, *Green Revolutions Reconsidered: The Rural World of Contemporary Punjab* (New Delhi: Oxford University Press, 2001). For its effects, Cynthia Hewitt de Alcantara, *Modernizing Mexican Agriculture: Socioeconomic Implications of Technological Change, 1940–1970* (Geneva: United Nations Research Institute for Social Development, 1976); and Gordon Conway, *The Doubly Green Revolution: Food for All in the Twenty-First Century* (Ithaca, NY: Cornell University Press, 1997). On food politics, Philip Raikes, *Modernising Hunger: Famine, Food Surplus and Farm Policy in the EEC and Africa* (London: James Currey, 1988); Jean Drèze and Amartya Sen (eds), *The Political Economy of Hunger*, 3 vols. (Oxford: Clarendon Press, 1990); and John H. Perkins, *Geopolitics and the Green Revolution: Wheat, Genes, and the Cold War* (New York: Oxford University Press, 1997).

Chapter 12

# McDonaldization and its discontents

With more than 70 billion hamburgers served by the year 2000, McDonald's restaurants are among the most pervasive and successful consumer icons in U.S. history. From its origins in suburban California, the chain exemplified the post-war society of abundance, with dependable food served quickly and cheaply in a family-oriented environment. As democracy became congruent with choice in the marketplace, fast food restaurants of all kinds proliferated on street corners and interstates throughout the land. The industry's annual sales of $100 billion accounted for half of the money spent on food prepared outside the home, or a quarter of the total spent on food in the U.S.

Yet the amazing success of the fast food industry within contemporary society has raised worries, as standardization increasingly replaces local cuisines with the artificial choices of "value menus" that are virtually the same at every chain. Meanwhile, the creation of so-called McJobs has deskilled restaurant labor to the point that workers, often earning below the minimum wage, perform no active role in food preparation but simply respond to the commands of machines, even as customers take over the jobs of waiting and busing tables. Many fear also that subliminal advertising of high-fat hamburgers and French fries has contributed to a growing epidemic of obesity. At the international level, McDonald's has become a focus of protest against U.S. imperial power.

## Fast food in the United States

The fast food industry achieved its success by following important trends in twentieth-century U.S. social history. Standardized hamburger flipping and French frying, like the automobile assembly line of Henry Ford, grew out of time and motion studies conducted in the early 1900s by industrial efficiency expert Frederick Taylor. The rise of an automobile culture and the post-war suburbanization of the middle class, in turn, created a tremendous demand for restaurants that catered to a society on the move. By the end of the century, the omnipresence of the media industry facilitated not only the growth of commercial brands but also interconnections between them, so that Hollywood movies generated advertisements for fast food chains.

The contemporary fast food restaurant design, differing only superficially from one chain to the next, evolved from a diverse line of eateries. Harvey House restaurants, built along transcontinental railroads in the nineteenth century, set the standard for providing reliable food to travelers; indeed, prim "Harvey girl" waitresses helped bring civilized dining to the "Wild West." In the 1920s, the urban White Castle chain gave respectability to the hamburger, formerly associated with greasy spoon cafés and itinerant stands, by serving it in sparkling clean, fairy tale surroundings. A decade later, Howard Johnson began locating franchises along highways, with gleaming orange roofs so that customers could see them from a distance. Diners also appeared on roadsides, often in streamlined metallic buildings featuring drive-through windows or carhop service.

The original McDonald's offered curbside service in 1930s' San Bernardino, California, but tired of a teenage, male clientele, brothers Richard and Maurice McDonald fired all their carhop waitresses in 1948 and revolutionized the fast food industry. They expanded the kitchen space while cutting down the menu to hamburgers, fries, and shakes – foods that could be eaten without utensils. Standardizing every burger with the same combination of ketchup, mustard, onions, and two pickles, plus greater division of labor and the use of disposable paper cups and sacks, allowed McDonald's to offer low prices. Profits followed from high customer volume, as families replaced the teenagers who formerly lingered in the restaurant. Finally, the brothers designed the distinctive arches, lit by neon at night, to make the restaurant visible from the road.

The McDonald brothers' concept proved highly profitable, but it was a traveling kitchen supply salesman, Ray Kroc, who built the fast food empire. Impressed by the volume of business at the San Bernardino restaurant, Kroc purchased the right to franchise the McDonald's system in 1954. Franchise holders, although independent businessmen, were kept under close control to ensure uniform quality. Hamburger University, founded in 1961, sought to heighten professionalism and loyalty among managers, sending them out with "ketchup in their veins."

From the beginning, McDonald's faced fierce competition, both for hamburgers and in the broader fast food market. Burger King had begun franchising already in 1953, and many considered their broiled burgers superior to McDonald's fried variety. Rivals also applied the techniques of industrial efficiency to other foods, including fried chicken, tacos, pizza, and ice cream parlors. Nevertheless, by the 1970s, McDonald's dominated the industry, a position that has continued into the twenty-first century. By this time the market had become so saturated with fast food restaurants that new branches were opening inside airports, stores, and school cafeterias, even as many local leaders sought to restrict their expansion.

## Global reach

Fast food chains also spread around the world, although standardized hamburgers triggered vastly different reactions among local cultures. McDonald's led this global growth, opening restaurants in Canada, Japan, Australia, and Western Europe in the late 1960s and the early 1970s, followed by Latin America, Asia, and the former Communist bloc in succeeding decades. To avoid criticism of "cultural imperialism," the chain went to great lengths to establish local sources of supply and to give franchise holders considerable autonomy. Contrary to the downscale associations of fast food in the United States, these restaurants became the preserve of relatively affluent diners, although few went as far as the candle-lit restaurants in Rio de Janeiro serving champagne with Big Macs.

The arrival of McDonald's in Asia illustrates the diversity of cultural reactions toward fast food. When the chain came to Japan in 1971, it appealed primarily to young people eager for Western fashions. The local manager even claimed, improbably: "If we eat McDonald's hamburgers and potatoes for a thousand years, we will become taller, our skin will become white, and our hair will be blonde." Exotic visions of America also contributed to McDonald's success in Beijing two decades later, but the Chinese found most appealing such seemingly insignificant but nevertheless democratizing experiences as waiting in the same line with everyone else and the novelty of clean public bathrooms. In India, dietary restrictions forced the company to make significant changes to the menu, removing beef and substituting Vegetable McNuggets. Moreover, these attitudes changed over time; a new generation in Hong Kong has grown up with McDonald's and no longer considers it to be foreign.

Europeans, by contrast, often dismissed fast food as an upstart assault on Western civilization. A 1989 protest against the opening of a McDonald's restaurant in Rome led to the founding of the Slow Food movement dedicated to preserving the leisure of delicious, regional cuisines from a workaholic society that made fast food seem appealing. French Minister of Culture Jack Lang oversaw the creation of a National Council of Culinary Arts to protect the culinary patrimony. "I'm no fan of hamburgers," he told reporters. Sheep farmer José Bové went further by demolishing a McDonald's restaurant under construction in the town of Millau, for which he was sentenced to three months in jail. Nevertheless, "McDo," as it is called in France, is the chain's most profitable European subsidiary, with more than 1,000 restaurants.

The most serious blow to McDonald's public relations was self-inflicted, when the company sued two British environmental activists for libel in 1994. Dave Morris and Helen Steel had distributed a pamphlet accusing the company of abuses ranging from tropical deforestation to underpaying employees. The McLibel case, as it became known, humiliated the company, all the more so when the defendants refused to retract their claims in a settlement offered by the company. Although the court ultimately found them guilty of some instances of libel, many of their accusations turned out to be true, damaging the company's reputation.

Yet an even greater challenge to McDonald's global markets came from local competitors offering rival versions of fast food. These chains were not only successful in their home territory, but often acquired their own global presence. Nando's, a Mozambican chicken franchise specializing in a spicy Peri Peri sauce, spread first to South Africa, where it claimed Portuguese origins after the former colonial power. The company later expanded across the Indian Ocean to Australia, inspiring numerous imitators. Meanwhile in Hong Kong, purveyors of Chinese-style fast food had regained 70 percent of the market from international hamburger chains by the turn of the century. Even McDonald's acknowledged the global limits of its hamburger model by purchasing competitors in other sectors of the fast food market.

## The obesity epidemic

Fast and industrial processed foods have also been held responsible for a spectacular growth in the number of overweight people around the world. The incidence of obesity began to climb in the United States in the late 1970s, and within two decades a full third of the population weighed at least 20 percent more than what doctors considered optimum. Nor was this trend limited to McDonald's homeland; by the end of the century, 15–20 percent of Western Europeans were significantly overweight, and in Eastern Europe the figure rose to 40–50 percent. Even Japanese rates of obesity climbed above 10 percent. Thus, a new set of health risks offset the benefits of industrial food production in the rich world. Moreover, diabetes and heart disease also spread to impoverished countries still suffering from anemia and malnutrition. By the year 2000, up to 300 million people worldwide were estimated to be obese.

The food industry has been haunted by its success in pushing ever greater consumption of fatty and sweet foods. In 2002, two overweight teenagers sued McDonald's for making them fat, and a popular documentary film called *Super Size Me* won critical acclaim. As the lawsuit made its way through the courts, declining profits forced to the company to add more healthy alternatives to its menu. An "Adult Happy Meal," marketed briefly, comprised a salad, bottled water, and a pedometer. Chains offering alternatives to high-fat burgers and fries, such as deli sandwiches and "Fresh Mex" burritos, benefited from McDonald's distress.

Indeed, the growing disparity between actual body size and ideals portrayed in the media racked up billions of dollars of annual sales for weight-loss clinics and purveyors of reducing drugs and low-calorie food and drinks. Drastic medical procedures such as gastric-bypass surgery, stapling the stomach, also became increasingly common. Rival expert claims about the benefits of high carbohydrates and low fats – or the opposite – as well as vitamins, preservatives, and additives, further perplexed consumers, contributing to the sale of diet foods and supplements with dubious health benefits.

Transnational marketing and media have helped diffuse poor diets and unrealistic attitudes about body size globally. Media personalities, fashion models, and beauty pageant contestants are uniformly slim around the world. At the same time, consumption of sugar and fat has become increasingly widespread, even among populations that cannot afford regular sources of animal protein. The dietary transition from peasant cuisines based on whole grains and legumes to an industrial diet of meat and refined carbohydrates has thus been sidetracked in many developing countries. Consequently, people have begun to suffer the diseases of affluence while still receiving inadequate nutrients on a daily basis.

## Conclusion

Both apologists and opponents have at times exaggerated the significance of McDonald's in shaping contemporary eating habits. The ubiquity of fast food in schools is certainly cause for concern, but the obesity epidemic must also be attributed to declining levels of exercise, no doubt aggravated by the process of deindustrialization, which has reduced physical activity among working-class people, who are most at risk. Those seeking to restrict the advertising and sale of fast food implicitly argue that people cannot be responsible for their own actions and that parents cannot make decisions for their own children. Likewise, although travelers may find the bland uniformity of golden arches in every country to be disturbing, the locals themselves may welcome the opportunity to eat something new and different. Protests of burger-Luddite José Bové notwithstanding, French cuisine has little to fear from the spread of McDonald's because fast food chains and local restaurants cater to quite different markets. Perhaps the real goal should be that all options, fast food and haute cuisine, like different ethnic foods, should flourish in pluralistic societies.

## Further reading

The best survey of fast food is John A. Jakle and Keith A. Sculle, *Fast Food: Roadside Restaurants in the Automobile Age* (Baltimore, MD: Johns Hopkins University Press, 1999). Critiques include Eric Schlosser, *Fast Food Nation: The Dark Side of the All-American Meal* (New York: Houghton Mifflin, 2001); and George Ritzer, *The McDonaldization Thesis* (London: Sage, 1998). On globalization, James L. Watson (ed.), *Golden Arches East: McDonald's in East Asia* (Stanford, CA: Stanford University Press, 1997); and Rick Fantasia, "Fast Food in France," *Theory and Society* 24 (1995): 201–43. For health concerns, see Peter N. Stearns, *Fat History: Bodies and Beauty in the Modern West* (New York: New York University Press, 1997).

# Chapter 13

# Culinary pluralism

Although the fascist horrors of World War II discredited theories of racial supremacy, periodic nationalist revivals continued throughout the twentieth century. The unraveling of European colonialism spurred decades of conflictual nation-building in Asia and Africa, followed in the late 1980s by the collapse of Communism and revived ethnic conflict in Eastern Europe. Even in stable democracies of Western Europe, the Americas, and Australasia, nationalist demagogues enflamed popular fears of contamination by new waves of labor migrants. As nations sought to define and control their boundaries in an increasingly complex world, eating provided a situation in which ethnic groups could gain acceptance or suffer exclusion in a particularly visceral fashion.

Decolonization offered great expectations to the people of Asia and Africa, but European nationalist models proved ill-suited to social conditions in former colonies. World War II weakened the imperial grip of Britain, France, and other European powers, and military attempts to prolong the occupations provoked bitter and futile wars. Even where independence came peacefully, the new leaders inherited political and economic systems designed for imperial exploitation rather than self-government. Ethnic homelands and colonial boundaries were particularly incongruous in Africa, but rather than re-draw the map, leaders sought to forge national identities through civic education, or failing that, through military means. Campaigns of ethnic cleansing killed millions around the world while displacing millions more. Former colonial powers gained another opportunity to "consume" their former subjects as refugees established ethnic restaurants in the metropolis; Vietnamese restaurants, for example, proliferated in communities across the United States after the fall of Saigon in 1975.

Economic integration also raised concerns about citizenship and ethnic minorities. Throughout the world, regions undergoing industrialization or engaged in agribusiness depended on labor migrants, but the presence of foreigners often ignited fears and resentments among residents. The switch to female-dominated migration, prompted by the rise of service work and restrictive immigration laws privileging family reunification, paradoxically fueled xenophobic fears as jobs for transient male workers seemingly were taken by families with strange-smelling foods and unfamiliar religious practices. Guest worker programs and tacit reliance on illegal immigrants, which exploited migrants economically without offering them hope of citizenship, became increasingly common.

Another paradox arose from the simultaneous growth of immigration restrictions and tourist interest in foreign cultures. The explosion of cookbook publishing encouraged authors to search out increasingly exotic cuisines, even as the consumption of food at home plummeted in wealthy countries. Books often served more as travel guides than kitchen aids, a pattern repeated on television cooking shows, where celebrity chefs competed to provide novelty and entertainment. Some programs specialized in foods considered bizarre to Western viewers; the macho hosts literally consumed alien cultures as a form of neocolonial conquest. Yet ordinary citizens of privileged nations too seldom reflected on the circumstances that brought, for example, Ethiopian food to the United States at a time when people were starving outside Addis Ababa.

## Postcolonial cuisines

In former colonies, as in nineteenth-century Europe, cuisine offered a significant contribution to the cultural project of nation building. As urban middle classes sought to forge a sense of national identity, cookbooks, restaurants, and even street corner vendors provided a non-threatening venue for crossing ethnic and class boundaries. Women, who were often excluded from formal politics, could find a particular sense of participation in the larger national community by helping to create a common cuisine. Nevertheless, aspiring kitchen nationalists faced difficult questions of just which foods to include in the national menu, and whether the sharing of foods would encourage other forms of cross-cultural exchange. Even more important in the long term, they had to find ways of translating domestic nationalism into more active forms of citizenship.

As nationalists sought to unify diverse vernacular traditions and to nation-alize elite cuisines, they often turned to European cultural patterns by default. In India, following independence, middle-class women began writing large numbers of cookbooks exploring regional differences. Foods had traditionally marked caste boundaries, and the sharing of dishes demonstrated a democratic acceptance of fellow citizens. To reach a pan-ethnic audience, authors generally wrote these volumes in English, illustrating the unique challenges faced by nationalist leaders in former colonies. Cookbooks also began appearing in Africa, but government provisioning policies had perhaps the greatest role in forging the national cuisine. Because cooking traditions were often relatively egalitarian, without considerable distinctions in the types of foods eaten by chiefs and subjects, elite ideals often were drawn from the cuisines of colonial rulers.

Few foods have acquired the status of national symbols in such a deliberate fashion as the Israeli adoption of falafel. These chickpea fritters, originally prepared by Arabs and sold from street corner stands, first gained popularity with young Jewish settlers in 1920s' Palestine. Following independence in 1948, and the influx of European Jews escaping the Holocaust, falafel was embraced as a unifying national icon that appealed to both Ashkenazi new-comers and long-established Sephardic Jews, without being the exclusive cultural property of either group. The dish also became popular among Diaspora Jews, further cementing their emotional ties to the Israeli homeland. By the 1970s, Jewish cookbooks included falafel recipes that made no mention of their Arab origins, which led many Palestinians to resent the appropriation of their dish.

Tourism and migration likewise helped create novel, often competing versions of national cuisines. In both developing countries and industrial powers alike, these foods offered powerful means of claiming or denying citizenship.

## Food and citizenship

Guaranteeing basic human rights remains a fundamental challenge for con-temporary societies, as they confront their invariably multi-ethnic nature. In this quest for social justice, food offers a valuable space for learning to appreciate cultural difference. Nevertheless, such an inclusive attitude cannot arise from simply treating lunch at an ethnic restaurant as an exotic tourist adventure, valued for sheer novelty, without a corresponding interest in the cultures that created these foods. It is therefore heartening that in the United States, for example, Tex-Mex burritos and Vietnamese spring rolls have gained legitimacy, a form of cultural citizenship, just as in earlier times hot dogs and spaghetti helped win acceptance for German and Italian Americans. Such culinary openness has been equally dramatic in contemporary Australia, as it seeks to construct a national identity bridging Europe and Asia. Yet under the Southern Cross, as elsewhere, the blinders of racism impede the ideals of pluralist democracy.

For nearly two centuries, Australian food was defined primarily by the colonial legacy, and only in the late 1970s did liberal immigration policies help to create an internationally acclaimed cuisine known as "Mod Oz." In the eighteenth century, Britain claimed the continent under the spurious legal doctrine of *terra nullis* (empty land), which simply ignored the aboriginal societies dating back some 40,000 years. From the beginning, settlers rejected the natives and their foods, depending instead on spoiled biscuit and other imports from Britain. Chinese cooks had arrived by the mid-nineteenth century, but their patrons were ill-prepared for anything more adventuresome than kidney pie and the occasional visit to a chop suey joint. Southern European restaurants appeared in the post-war era, but subsequent Asian migrants had an even greater impact on Australian cooking. In 1975, several years before Pacific fusion washed up on the shores of California, Malaysian-born Chinese chef Cheong Liew inaugurated East-Meets-West cuisine in his Adelaide restaurant Neddy's – although home cooks in multi-ethnic families no doubt had experimented with similar blends even earlier. Nor was this influence limited to trendy restaurants and ethnic enclaves; Asian ingredients, flavors, and cooking techniques spread to ordinary European restaurants, bistros, and pubs. Supermarket shoppers can purchase Chinese cabbage and Indonesian chili sauce, then find recipes in mainstream women's magazines. The incredible proliferation of Thai restaurants since 1980 strikingly demonstrates this pan-ethnic appeal. By 2000, about 8 percent of the restaurants in Sydney served Thai cuisine, when the census counted fewer than 30,000 Thais, a fraction of 1 percent of the city's population.

"Mod Oz" chefs fortuitously gained international renown as culinary tourism became increasingly significant to the broader tourist industry. As the quality of food became increasingly important in vacation planning, the Australian Tourist Commission promoted upscale Sydney restaurants and Adelaide wine tours to entice visitors down under. The government of Thailand meanwhile created a program called Global Thai to facilitate the spread of the national cuisine by exporting authentic ingredients and helping chefs become established around the world.

Even as Asian newcomers were seated at the Mod Oz table, Australia's earliest inhabitants remained marginalized. A culinary version of *terra nullis* held that the aboriginal knowledge offered nothing of value to Australian cooking, even as courts began to redress the injustice of past land appropriations. Native foods were instead considered a raw material, to be developed by chefs from more advanced countries. Apart from barramundi fish and Morton Bay Bugs (a delicious crustacean, notwithstanding the name), one of the first native ingredients to undergo such gentrification was the *witjuti* (witchetty) grub, sold as canned soup since the 1970s. Within a few decades, trendy chefs were serving kangaroo steak with wattle-seed mash. Nevertheless, aboriginal influences met with greater resistance than Asian dishes; one study concluded that the greatest value of native resources lay in identifying "flavour/aroma components" for industrial processed foods rather than harvesting actual plants and animals that might benefit aboriginals economically. Racial exclusion thus continued to frustrate efforts to build pluralistic societies.

## Conclusion

While it is difficult to foretell the future course of culinary pluralism, past encounters between culinary nation-builders and migrant cooks suggest that initial fear and rejection will be followed by familiarity and acceptance. The aging of populations in industrial nations will create ever-greater demands for outside labor. Political campaigns against labor migration may increase the levels of exploitation, but they are seldom intended to exclude workers outright. Restaurants remain an important area for such labor, although whether the spread of these foods will benefit the vendors remains uncertain. Industrial rationalization has often alienated cuisines from their ethnic communities. Fast food versions of Mexican cooking in the United States, for example, bear little resemblance to the foods either of Mexico or of Mexican Americans. Yet the very growth of such ersatz industrial foods seems likely to generate interest in more authentic versions of the cuisine, providing a space for local identities to flourish.

## Further reading

Arjun Appadurai, "How to Make a National Cuisine: Cookbooks in Contemporary India," *Comparative Studies in Society and History* 30 (January 1988): 3–24; Ivan Cusak, "African Cuisines: Recipes for Nation Building," *Journal of African Cultural Studies* 13(2) (2000): 207–25; Yael Raviv, "Falafel: A National Icon," *Gastronomica* 3(3) (Summer 2003): 20–5; Cherry Ripe, *Goodbye Culinary Cringe* (Sydney: Allen & Unwin, 1996); Donna R. Gabaccia, *We Are What We Eat: Ethnic Food and the Making of Americans* (Cambridge, MA: Harvard University Press, 1998); Elspeth Probyn, *Carnal Appetites: FoodSexIdentities* (London: Routledge, 2000); and Lisa Heldke, *Exotic Appetites: Ruminations of a Food Adventurer* (New York: Routledge, 2003).

# Conclusion

Twice in history, the human race has fundamentally transformed its source of sustenance, and hence its place in the world. Thousands of years ago, the invention of agriculture paradoxically narrowed dietary options from the ever-changing bounty of the hunter–gatherer to the repetitive harvest of the sedentary farmer. Nevertheless, food surpluses also led to the formation of complex societies by supporting kings, priests, merchants, and artists – including culinary artists, who devised novel ways of preparing otherwise monotonous grains. In the nineteenth century, industrialization initiated equally significant changes in food habits and social relations. Once again, humanity learned to make more from less, producing greater quantities from fewer varieties of foodstuffs. Yet in contrast to agrarian societies, contemporary surpluses have been achieved by radically separating production from consumption, thereby straining the social connections between cooks and eaters.

Food and modernity have shared a complex, often troubled relationship. Mass production transformed eating habits, but food also played a crucial role in the rise of industry. The spice trade inspired Columbus and other European mariners in their voyages of discovery, and the introduction of foodstuffs from the Americas fueled population growth, thereby providing labour for early factories. Food businesses also contributed directly to Europe's economic take-off, and industrial processed foods, from cans of delivered ham to bottles of Coca-Cola, ultimately helped to incorporate traditional cultures into the modern global economy. Each step in this sweeping chain of socio-economic transition was negotiated at the local level – indeed, resisted fiercely in many cases – as individuals sought to shape change to their own advantage.

In the study of cross-cultural exchange, world historians must therefore consider multiple levels of analysis, connecting global economic processes with local cultural nuances. The most fundamental aggregates of world population result in part from dietary choices made at the domestic level. Methods of food preparation can also shape gender roles and social hierarchies. Meanwhile, the politics of food provisioning connects rulers to subjects through bonds of trust, or failing that, through outbursts of violence and food riots. Thus, food history is an important field of research bringing large-scale trends home, literally, to the dinner table.

In the cross-cultural exchange of foods, certain general trends emerge. Perhaps the most basic of these rules is the conservatism of food habits and the desire of people to maintain their traditional sources of sustenance. The extensive African influence on the foods of Brazil, the Caribbean, and the southern United States provides a testament to the tenacity of slave cooks in preserving their culture under extreme circumstances. A corollary of this observation is that new foods tend to gain acceptance within a culinary system most readily when they are similar to existing items. Cooks in China and the Middle East devised acceptable ways of preparing New World crops as porridge and noodles more rapidly than did those in Europe, who preferred raised breads. Another consequence of this general conservatism is that novel foods tend to be insinuated at the margins of culinary systems and by individual cooks. For example, colonized Africans ate European foods such as canned ham and tea as a snack after they had finished their regular meal of porridge. Nevertheless, ceremonial foods can also be a focus of interest by those attempting to transform a society. During the Spanish conquest of Mexico, Catholic priests sought to introduce wheat bread into religious ceremonies to break the religious connections with former maize gods. Moreover, these diverse influences can lead to peculiar culinary mixtures. Migrants in the contemporary world often juxtapose distinct culinary ceremonies as a way of asserting citizenship in their new country while maintaining connections to the ancestral homeland, for example, by serving lasagna at Thanksgiving dinner or eating birthday cake at the end of a Chinese banquet. Indeed, the complexity of culinary change renders military terms such as triumph or resistance less useful as metaphors than biological notions of adaptation and hybrids.

The history of food politics has manifested equally complex patterns. Agrarian societies adopted widely different approaches to guaranteeing urban subsistence, ranging from the Confucian and Inca zeal for civil service to classical Mediterranean and Islamic notions of private charity. Effective government administration is crucial to the success of provisioning, even in societies that depend largely on the market. Yet food shortages seem to inspire the greatest degree of popular unrest when societies pass through transitional periods and new attitudes emerge regarding the boundaries between state responsibility and market functions. The rise of free-market liberalism in eighteenth-century Europe provided one such instance of instability, and neo-liberal attempts to spread such attitudes to developing countries have triggered similar riots in the twentieth century. Government oversight over food supplies remains important even in industrial societies, where surpluses have redirected the focus of regulation from ensuring adequate supplies to guaranteeing the healthfulness of foods. Thus, the tension between market efficiency and state intervention has no more been resolved in the modern West than it was in China's Qing Dynasty.

The transition to modernity is seemingly the story of ever-widening Western influence – if not hegemony. France has set the standards for elite dining ever since the seventeenth century, and as likely as not, the most exclusive restaurants in any major city of the contemporary world will serve French cuisine. The global masses have also been subjected to the manufactured tastes of industrial foods from Europe and the United States. Even in the most remote villages, subsistence farmers have incorporated processed sugars and fats into their diets. Western attitudes about food have been equally influential around the world. The carnivorous diet idealized by feudal lords of the medieval era has become a source of global desire through the icon of the McDonald's hamburger. Europe's preferred grain, wheat, has also gained cachet throughout Africa and the Americas, while maize, sorghum, and many other non-Western staples have been relegated to the status of animal feed in Europe.

Five centuries of imperial rule have weighed heavily in this cultural balance, making European peculiarities appear to be global standards. The tropical plantation system was created to provide Europe with abundant supplies of sugar, cacao, and other commodities, which subsequently became staple foods in non-Western countries, often to the detriment of nutritional health. Even post-colonial elites imbibed the cultural prejudices of the continent while studying in European schools. Moreover, current development efforts such as the Green Revolution now appear simply as updated versions of the nineteenth-century imperialist "civilizing mission."

Yet globalization is not a one-way process, passing from the elites to the masses, nor is it merely a synonym for Westernization. A succession of imperial agents, from Spanish conquistadors to British sahibs and U.S. development experts, have believed their own culture to be superior and sought to impose it on subject peoples. By contrast, the natives have viewed the imperial menu not as a *prix fixe* to be followed slavishly, but instead have chosen *à la carte* those items that prove useful and that fit within their existing culture. Moreover, culinary exchanges often run in the opposite direction, with colonial masters enjoying the foods of their subjects. Likewise, in early modern Japan, the samurai elite came to embrace a popular cuisine of soba and sushi. Even metropolitan French cuisine has relied on the inventiveness of working-class cooks from the provinces to revitalize itself. In the past century, proletarian migrations have arguably done more to globalize eating habits than have multinational food corporations. Lively ethnic restaurants from San Francisco to Sydney and from Buenos Aires to Berlin exemplify a working-class cosmopolitanism that has inspired envy among more "sophisticated" elites.

Continued European culinary dominance seems ever more questionable in the new millennium. Awareness has grown of the unsustainable nature of current livestock production, never mind the impossibility of extending the carnivorous Western diets to billions in the developing world. Together with the current epidemic of obesity, this knowledge has prompted growing numbers in the West to replace meat with legumes. Change has also been facilitated by the international popularity of food from such countries as Mexico, Thailand, and India, where French culinary modernity – subtle, "natural" tastes – never replaced the vibrant flavors of spices and chiles. Thus, the Pacific Rim rather than Europe may well inspire the global cuisine of the future.

Despite dramatic change over time, a fundamental continuity stands out, the persistent inequality of food distribution and nutritional health. In agrarian societies since the Neolithic age, the elite have grown fat on the surpluses produced by farm laborers. The majority of the world's population still lives in such societies, and nearly a billion people remain malnourished. By contrast, the Western world began to develop new understandings of nutrition and health as food supplies became more secure in the early modern age. In the nineteenth century, Europeans harnessed nutritional science to the new global division of labor, using dietary superiority as a justification for imperial conquest abroad and for racial discrimination against migrant workers at home. The superabundance of foods in the twentieth century reversed those medical beliefs; obesity went from being a sign of affluence to a grave health risk, one borne most heavily by the poor. Consumer arithmetic was likewise upended, and animal fats appeared cheap and plentiful while organic produce became rare and expensive. The modern paradox that only the rich can afford to eat like peasants simply perpetuates the age-old inequality of food provisioning.

# Index

citizenship 63–64, 67, 69, 83, 91, 113, 114, 119

civilization 11, 13; barbarism contrasted 8, 9, 11, 15; "civilizing mission" 69, 71, 74, 77, 120; culinary definitions 13, 71, 72, 109; origins 4, 8, 118

class distinction: Britain 18, 34, 37–38, 73; China 6, 8, 9–10, 15, 68; food as marker 2, 4, 35–36, 52, 64, 118, 120; France 18, 34–37, 65; Inca 22; Japan 39–40; Mexico 20, 21, 23, 66; Middle East 8; Rome 12

Coen, Jan Pieterszoon 30, 33

coffeehouses 18, 34, 38–39

Cold War 87, 91, 96–98, 100, 101, 105, 107

Colombani, J. A. 71

Columbian Exchange 2, 5, 19–25, 32, 42, 55, 71

Columbus, Christopher 19, 23, 118

commensality 2, 11, 12; see also banquets

commodities 17, 51, 55, 120

communism 88, 91, 94–95, 98, 104, 113

Confucius 9, 10

Congo 28, 75

consumerism 5, 7, 18, 51, 56, 58, 59–61, 88, 89, 97

cookbooks: Africa 114; Argentina 83; Britain 37, 72; China 15; contemporary 114; France 35–36, 52, 64; India 114; Italy 25, 66; Japan 40; Jewish 115; Medieval European 12, 15, 27, 34; Mexico 66; Middle East 15, 41; Rome 12; Vietnam 74

Côte d'Ivoire 28, 77

Crusades 14

Cuba 80, 81

cuisine: Chinese 10, 11, 68, 69; court 5, 10, 16, 39, 64, 68, 69, 74; French 3, 5, 35, 36, 41, 64, 66, 69, 75, 112, 120; fusion 6, 115–116; haute 3, 4, 5, 10, 12, 15, 78; national 5, 6, 52, 63–69, 74, 84, 85, 114–115; Persian 14; popular 34, 39–40, 120; regional 11, 14, 65, 66, 69, 74, 82

culinary blending: Americas 32, 80–84; China 11; Mexico 21; Middle East 15; Vietnam 74–75

culinary conservatism 21, 23–25, 51, 60, 61, 68, 73, 77, 82, 119

culinary culture: Africa 15, 28–29, 32, 67, 76; Britain 5, 37–38, 69, 72; China 9–11, 68, 74; France 5, 35–37, 64–66, 69, 74; Italy 11–13, 15, 30, 82–84; India, 1–2, 15, 71–73, 121; Japan 34, 39–40, 120; Mexico 1–2, 20, 67, 117, 121; Middle East 5, 8, 13–15, 30; Thailand 68–69, 74, 121; United States 52, 108–112; Vietnam 74–75

culinary knowledge 24, 55, 118

cultural hegemony 6, 120

cultural imperialism 6, 110

Czech Republic 63

Delhi 15

democracy 5, 38–39, 67, 87, 98, 104, 105, 108, 110

demographic transition 19, 101

Desmoulins, Camille 39

diabetes 111

Dias, Bartolomeu 30

Díaz del Castillo, Bernal 21

dictatorship 87, 91, 93–95, 98

Diderot, Denis 39

dietary laws: Hindu 15, 73, 75, 110; Jewish 8, 15, 60; Muslim 14, 73; see also taboos

diets: China 10, 13; fads 1; humoral 10, 12–13, 27, 36; McDiets 6; Middle East 13; modern 5, 6, 10, 36, 52, 55, 101, 120; transition 112; vegetarian 1, 2, 15, 20, 73, 110; weight loss 111–112

diffusion of crops: colonialism and 17, 47, 73, 74, 119; migration and 52, 81, 83, 119; negotiation of 19, 23; and population 3, 5, 18, 24; trade and 2, 13, 15

Djenne 29

domestication of crops: China 9; Middle East 8; South America 2, 21

Dominican Republic 67

Routledge History

## Migration in World History

*Patrick Manning*

From the spread of *Homo sapiens* onward, migration has been a major factor in human development. This wide-ranging survey traces the connections among regions brought about by the movements of people, diseases, crops, technology and ideas. Drawing on examples from a wide range of geographical regions and thematic areas, Manning presents a useful overview, including:

- earliest human migrations and the first domestication of major plants and animals
- the rise and spread of major language groups such as Indo-European, Afro-Asiatic, Niger-Congo, Indo-Pacific, Sino-Tibetan, Altaic, and Amerindian
- trade patterns including the early Silk Road and maritime trade in the Mediterranean and Indian Ocean
- the increasing impact of maritime and overland migrations on areas of life such as religion and family
- the effect of migration on empire and industry between 1700 and 1900
- the resurgence of migration in the later twentieth century, including movement to cities, refugees and diasporas.

Hb: 0–415–31148–9 Pb: 0–415–31147–0

## Childhood in World History

*Peter N. Stearns*

Childhood exists in all societies, though there is huge variation in the way it is socially constructed across time and place. Studying childhood historically greatly advances our understanding of what childhood is about and a world history focus permits some of the broadest questions to be asked.

In *Childhood in World History* Peter N. Stearns focuses on childhood in several ways:

- childhood across change – the shift from hunting and gathering to an agricultural society and the impact of civilization and the emergence of major religions
- new and old debates about the distinctive features of Western childhood, including child labour
- the emergence of a modern, industrial pattern of childhood in the West, Japan and communist societies, including a focus on education and economic dependence
- globalization and the spread of child-centred consumerism.

This historical perspective highlights the gains but also the divisions and losses for children across the millennia.

Hb: 0–415–35232–0 Pb: 0–415–35233–9

Available at all good bookshops
For ordering and further information please visit:
www.routledge.com